Walking Back Home

Hiking the Pacific Crest Trail, Part I

Rick Rogers

This book is dedicated to my Family, Monica and Matthew, for letting me go, and even more surprisingly, letting me come home. I'd also like to thank Gina, for finding a way, and my other family and friends for their belief.

Cover photo by Rick Rogers

I have tried to recreate events, locales and conversations from my imperfect memories of them. In order to maintain their anonymity in some instances I have changed the names of individuals and places, I may have changed some identifying characteristics and details such as physical properties, occupations and places of residence.

Rick Rogers
Visit my website at www.http://geoduckyrick.blogspot.com/

Printed in the United States of America

First Printing: February 2019
Amazon Books

ISBN- 9781795465960

Foreword

This book covers the first half of my walk home on the Pacific Crest Trail. It's a long trail, so there's a lot of country to see, people to meet, stories to tell. I wanted to write a book that would be interesting to adults, but mostly I wanted something suitable for a fifth grader's book report. Even after editing, if all the country, people, and stories were put into one book, the page count would scare off all but the most over-achieving of them. The goal was to walk home from Palm Springs, California to Conway, Washington, leaving on April 5 and getting home on September 30. Plans were planned, arrangements arranged, courses of action acted upon. The master plan was executed to perfection up until I was deposited onto the trail April 5. And that was the last I ever saw or heard of it. I hope you enjoy...

Cast of Characters

I have tried to recreate events, locales and conversations from my imperfect memories of them. In some instances I have changed the names of individuals, places, or details.

Monica- My long-suffering wife and personal angel
Sheila- Pre-hike pen pal and first hiking partner
Glasses- Bestower of trail names
Ryegrass- John Muir reincarnation
Norm- Trail Angel Transport
Gaby- Bolivian Chef
DJ- Veteran PTSD hiker
Mr. Calamity- Trick knee
Toni- Looking for a hike
Art- Boat Captain
Buckwheat- Retired genius
Puzzles- Hiker with new PhD in Mathematics
Jeff & Cindy- Airbnb hosts in Wrightwood
Cool Breeze- My second hiking partner
Two Shakes- PCT trail names explained
Diane- Police recruit
Daryl- Veteran firefighter
Clem- Sedentary hiker
Ernesto- Sheepherder
Don & Emily- Living the dream
Chameleon- My third hiking partner
Houdini & Turtle Hair- Chameleon's second hiking partners
Karate Kid- Foot seamstress
Osprey- Quit the Trail for good
Kenny- Too busy to quit
Two-Tents- Shelter impairment syndrome
Fox Tail Guy- Waiter in Belden
Trashers- Mom & son litterbugs
Blue Dog- Internet troll
Kitty & Shoeless- Chameleon's first trail family
Brian- Catfishing guide hopeful
Dave- Retired burnin' nasties faller
Rubberchicken- My favorite hiking partner

Table of Contents

WHY?

The Willapa school library was usually missing its copy of the June 1971 National Geographic while I was a middle schooler. I read and reread the cover story following four guys that walked from Mexico to Canada on the newly established Pacific Crest Trail. I spent a lot of lunch periods revising gear checklists. I made backpacks from feed sacks and baling twine and carried canned peas and stuff through the woods for practice. I'd walk up and down a logging road where truckers had painted mile markers on trees, gauging my speed and mileage so I could fine tune my PCT itineraries. I determined that when my first chance came to go, I would.

That determination to go has never left. Every daydream; every time I wished I was somewhere else, it was hiking with those guys on the Nat Geo cover. It's surprising and a little irritating that my life's decisions and circumstances has had me waiting four and half decades for a responsible chance to go, but it's here now and I am thankful for it. Extremely thankful. My wife is supportive and at a stage in her career where she can take time off work to be a full-time parent. We have (we hope) a time window between caring for and burying parents, we have some money saved up, my feet and legs are still working OK, and the country hasn't yet devolved into anarchy. I've postponed the trip 45 consecutive seasons now, and at this age I've seen enough to know that another postponement could very well make it impossible.

So why am I going? Here I am, a late middle-aged guy going five months without a paycheck to walk 2,400 miles, sleep alone on the ground and eat noodles. I won't find myself out there, or find a new God, or a more enlightened meaning for life. I already know where I fit in the world. This isn't an exercise in self-discovery. For all the profound questions, I already have workable answers.

I'm going so I can see a lot of country. Breathe a lot of air. Cover a lot of ground. Take a lot of pictures. See if north slope trees there look like the ones here; if the birds sound the same, what the lichens look like. Just to see what walking the trail is like, really. I've been thinking about this trip for so long now, I'm curious to see if the trail is the way I imagine it is.

Or if the trail is more what that kid in Mrs. Hartwig's library imagined so long ago. So that's it really, why I'm going. I'm going to find out. Then I'll let you know.

SHEILA

Miles on Trail... 92

Leaving work, rain, and home construction behind was something I had been looking forward to for a long time. Leaving behind my family wasn't. The last couple weeks had been an event filled and emotional whirlwind and I knew that there would be time to process. Besides a deep gratitude, I was still thinking about family and friends that had been to my send-off party. Other than family (who's obligated) there were a half-dozen people that told me that they loved me. Humbling.

The original plan was to get on the trail from the Palm Springs tram, but two of my penpals I was supposed to meet up with had already bailed and the third was in Idyllwild and ready to go. So the trip started for me there at Humber Park, a side trail that climbs 3,600 feet or so in a couple hours. There was a lot of panting.

Sheila had wanted to start walking around noon or so, but I had started an hour earlier to have a more private parting. So I had some time for a nap at Saddle Junction where the trail meets the PCT at mile 179. Sheila was genuinely happy to see me there, dropped her pack to give me a hug. She's as big around as my leg and was soaking wet. She doesn't like sun, and won't abide sunscreen products so covers herself head to toe with Value Village attire. A floppy denim sun hat, a dark print shirt, brown corduroy pants, and woolen mittens. It was three in the afternoon, 80 degrees, and she had just climbed 3,600 feet.

"I'm so happy to see you! I brought you a book," she said. She pulled a two-pound novel out of her pack and handed it to me.

"Thanks so much, this is my favorite author. It's so thoughtful of you. I can't believe that you'd carry this extra weight up the hill for me," I said.

"It's nothing," she said. "Here, lift up my pack."

It weighed close to fifty pounds. Incredible. "What do you have in here?"

4

"Books, there was a great secondhand bookstore there. And good food. Most of your American food is so bad I won't eat it. Idyllwild had some good food stores so I stocked up."

"She must eat rocks and concrete," I thought.

There was another 1,000 feet to climb and few more miles to go for the night's camp.

"You must get rid of those walking sticks, I find them very distracting and annoying."

"They hold my tent up, " I said.

"Then you will walk behind me"

Sheila walked fast; no sticks, bent forward so her pack was almost parallel to the ground. She would raise her foot 3 or 4 inches higher than necessary for each step and then slam it hard down. From behind, she looked angry.

"Your panting is horrendous. It shows that your fitness level isn't where it needs to be for you to be here on the trail."

I told her that I might be better when I developed a trail routine, and asked about hers, since it seemed to be working.

"Sleep is important on the trail," she said. " I sleep till 10 or so, pack camp and walk 3 miles before breakfast. Then I stop and make coffee for breakfast, triple shot espresso. I won't drink weak coffee. Then I walk till about 5 and make camp."

We got to a campsite. "I must have level ground and cannot be disturbed by rustling or snoring. This will be my spot, and you will set your tent up over there." Then she went off to explore.

When she got back she said, "Put your things back in your pack, we aren't where I thought we were so we need to move up another mile or so."

A mile up the trail a group of hikers had tents up and were eating dinner. Sheila wanted to introduce me to everyone but I declined. I felt like being alone so I told Sheila I'd move up the trail a bit and see her at her coffee stop in the morning. That was a peaceful night.

Next morning, I packed my stuff and then killed a few hours waiting for Sheila to come make her coffee stop. Waiting for people that are late getting out of bed just gravels me. What the heck? Millions of kindergartners have already been put on school busses already, so what's the problem, I thought.

"Those other hikers ruined my sleep," she said when she got there. We talked about the wind warning from the weather forecast and that it would be best to 'get off the ridge' before night if possible. That would be a long day.

On the way down the ridge, I met a middle-aged friendly woman strolling down the trail.

"Hi, I'm Glasses. This is my third time hiking the PCT. Last year I made it almost to Kennedy Meadows before I found out that I'm allergic to mosquitoes. This time I will cover myself thoroughly with mud."

Glasses is a prodigious bestower of trail names and was keen to give me one. We talked some and it turned out that we had gone to the same school for a while. Her parents bought the dairy farm I grew up on, and for a time she lived in the house we had moved from. She knew my stepbrother and stepfather well.

"This is amazing that we should meet out here and I believe that everything happens for a reason with all my heart, don't you think?" she asked.

"Can't argue with that," I said. In my experience, people who believe that are continuously befuddled, disappointed, or in extreme cases, religious. I decided it would be best to go around her and make some miles before the winds came.

"It was nice meeting you!" she called after me. "When we meet again I will give you a trail name!"

"Not if I can help it," I thought, and if we never met again there really would be a reason for it.

"Why do you think I'm carrying this guitar to Canada?" He was an earnest looking twenty year old kid with black hair and glasses and a thin goatee. In addition to a loaded pack on his back, he had the handle of a guitar case in his hand. I thought about it a minute, because he seemed to really want an answer and I couldn't imagine he wanted to hear the obvious.

"Well, it's not like the damned thing is going to carry itself there," I said.

He beamed. "I've asked everyone I've met the same question and so far you're the only person to get it right. You couldn't imagine what most people say."

It was 90 degrees, the wind was gusting to 60, and we were halfway down a 22-mile grade. I really could imagine what most people would say. I traded one of my sticks for the guitar to see what it was like to carry it for a quarter mile or so. Unsurprisingly, it sucked.

Getting down the ridge to the alluvial fan was brutal. There was supposed to be a cache of water bottles halfway down, but when I got there it was empty. A lot of thirsty people trying to get off the ridge had been counting on that cache. At the bottom of the ridge was a throng of unhappy people around a water faucet. There was a metal sign on a short post near the faucet that read, 'Provided by Snow Creek Water Association'. There were a number of backpacks leaning against the short post, and by the look of several of the other hikers it looked like the sign was positioned perfectly to slice foreheads open.

"I've gotten a hotel room in Banning, but THERE'S NO UBER!", a wild eyed guy with a bleeding forehead yelled at me through the wind. People looked shell shocked, some were crying. Amidst the turmoil, guitar boy was strumming a new song he was making up on the spot.

"I have walked twenty miles for water, sweet water and will walk another hundred for ice cream, Jesus I swear."

My feet hurt but I walked another half mile or so away from the carnival, set up my tent, and got in out of the wind. I got a text from Sheila saying that she couldn't get off the ridge and was camping there. Also that she wanted me to text her back in the morning to see if she was still alive. I couldn't tell if she was being overly dramatic, or if this was another example of Australian humor. About 11 o'clock a particularly nasty gust partially lifted me and my tent off the ground, flung my tent stakes into the desert, and dropped me-now encased in a violent tube of tent fabric-back onto the ground. It was like being beaten with hiking sticks inside a wind sock in a hurricane. I've slept better. It wasn't so bad after I got most of the fluttery stuff underneath me, and got some good sleep till my bladder woke me.

Now this was an interesting puzzle. The winds weren't constant; they'd blast from one direction, and then instantly blast from another. So there was no direction I could point without spray-painting myself with aerosolized urine. Nor could I get off my stuff without the wind blowing it out into desert somewhere in the dark. So I used a water bottle.

Next morning the winds eased off a bit and I was able to call Monica with Google Duo. It's like Skype except works better on cell phones and is free.

"It looks windy there," she said when I got her.

I told her about the night, showed her how I had to sleep on top of the tent, and the partially filled water bottle.

"Are you going to keep drinking out of that? That's disgusting!" Then she switched her phone screen around to selfie-mirror mode so she didn't have to see it.

At my end, I was treated to a close-up view of her fingernail noodling away at an upper gumline. "This is why technology shouldn't be trusted to our hands," I thought.

Packing up, I found most of my tent stakes. The tip of a hiking stick had broken off in a grommet, but other than that all intact. This early in the morning it was the perfect temperature for walking, so I left without Sheila who was nine miles back. No sense in both of us walking through the desert in the heat of the day.

The people clustered around the water faucet looked like they had a rough night, except for one kid. "How do you like this?" he asked, brandishing an ice axe.

"Why didn't you just mail it to yourself at Kennedy Meadows, Stupid?" asked a grouchy looking woman.

The kid looked back to me and said, "Cougars, man. Cougars are gonna eat her man, and I've got this!" I told him that she was probably packing heat. "Man," he said, backing away. "I'm walking down to the freeway and taking an Uber to the In-and-Out burger. Then I'm taking a big dump- the biggest, man."

"THERE'S NO UBER!", yelled the wild-eyed man.

The trail crossed the highway through a wash under a bridge where there was a little stockpile of hiker treats from Trail Angels and a message board and a couple Sharpies. "Welcome to Cabazon," said the message board. "This is your lowest elevation until you reach the Columbia River. Happy Trails and Good luck".

"Jesus is a Buddhist!" From a guy calling himself Shenanigans. "Dork," I thought and took an apple. From there the trail wound around a residential area and then up an arroyo towards the Mesa Wind Farm. This was one of the older original wind farms, and their turbines are mounted atop derricks, like skinny Eiffel towers rather than the more modern tower tubes. When I looked closer, I noticed that some of the derricks had no turbines on top.

A lot of them, actually. An alarming number of the bare derricks were twisted or mangled on top and some were bent like candy canes. I passed a sign that said: WARNING! WIND TURBINE AREA! BEWARE FLYING DEBRIS HAZARD! The sign was liberally dented by shrapnel. For Pete's sake. This was about halfway to the day's destination, the Whitewater Preserve, an old trout farm converted to a park with wading pools and camping. It was late morning and the heat was getting crazy again, over 90 degrees. I tried to imagine what it would be like sitting amongst the cactus and drinking a triple shot espresso. Insane, probably.

I knew I was getting close when I started meeting nice smelling people without backpacks on the trail. At one spot, called Canyon Overlook, I met a cheerful 50-ish Japanese couple. They stood there, squarely in the center of the trail, a rock wall on one side and a sheer drop off on the other. They were smiling, but not moving. So, each in turn, I'd put my hands on their shoulders and gently push their backs against the rock wall, then shuffle sideways with my backpack hanging out over empty space to get around them. They never resisted, never said anything, and smiled at me the whole time.

The Whitewater Preserve was a cool, shady peace of heaven in the desert. Camping for PCT hikers is free, so I set up in a shaded corner of a grassy field out of the way. There were restrooms with running water, so it was easy to have a shave, then back to my corner to have a nap.

"I'm Ryegrass, is that your tent?" I looked up and there was a short guy, 60ish, that looked for all the world like John Muir. He seemed pleased with the look. "Your tent is crooked and it's short."

"So are you," I thought and told him about the tip breaking off in the grommet.

"Yes, beginners are always snapping their tips off. It takes some experience to learn that you can't just jab them in to everything as you walk along. "

"I've had these over 20 years", I said.

"Well, you might figure it out if you stick with it. Hey, why do you have those carabiners on your pack? You could have saved a good ounce leaving them off. And you've shaved! You need to get used to having a beard, you'll see," he said stroking his.

"Ryegrass, I've tried. I really have, but I just can't get used to the idea of male pubic hair anywhere near my mouth. How did you get used to it?"

Ryegrass stomped off. A little later Sheila stomped over. She was soaking wet with sweat and still wearing the megaton backpack. She shook a wool-mittened finger at me. "I have walked twenty-three miles through a hell desert to catch you. We will talk in the morning." And then she stomped off.

It was another nice evening. I saw the kid with the ice axe and asked how it went at In-and-Out. "Plugged it, Man!" he said. "Their gonna need a Roto -Rooter and a f'ing fire truck to salvage that thing man!" We high-fived and I made dinner and went to bed.

In the morning, I bandaged and moleskinned my feet, had oatmeal, packed up, and went over towards Sheila' s tent where Ryegrass intercepted me.

"That woman hates you. And she's crazy." This seemed to bother him, as if I should only be hated by rational people.

"Why are you all packed up and ready to go?", Sheila asked, irritated. "You know my schedule."

"Yeah, I can't do that," I said. "I'm going to have to get through the desert to the next water before it's too hot." We decided that I'd go on ahead and we'd camp together that night.

It's nice to hike by yourself when you don't feel too alone. I carry a GPS unit that sends and receives text messages even if you're out of cell range. I got a few satellite texts to make me feel connected to home. I found water and shade after about 15 miles of desert, took the shoes and socks off my blistered feet and took a nap.

Sheila arrived a few hours later. "Put your things back in your pack, I will not camp here," she said. So I did, got behind her with my annoying hiking sticks and watched her little stomping feet go another mile or two up the trail until we came across a spot Sheila found more suitable. "You will camp here and I will camp there, but you must not snore, rustle, or wake me in the morning. I'm going to explore and we will speak tonight."

She left, and I got my tent up and kitchen stuff together. While I was treating water, Brian, a civil engineer turned massage therapist hiked in.

"Hey Rick, mind if I join you tonight?" "That'll be great," I said and pointed at the spot Sheila had picked for herself. Brian had his tent up and we were eating dinner and chatting when she came back.

"This is Brian," I said.

"I know who he is," she said, hands on hips. "That's my spot".

We decided that I would leave early again without waking anyone, but would stop when I got out of the desert and back into timber. It's weird hiking up out of a desert into a forest, the biomes can't decide where one should live and the other give way. I took a picture along the trail that had cactus, manzanita, wild oak, and pine trees all in the same spot. When I got into good solid pine forest, it seemed to me that everything was coming together for a good bathroom break.

Because it's one of the first things the non-hiking members of my family ask about, I thought I'd write about it here early on and get it out of the way.

So. Take a look at the items in the photo. Everything's there ready to go.

First, find a nice tree to lean against and at its base, dig a 6 inch diameter hole 8 inches deep with your trowel. When this is done, that's it for the trowel. It only digs in clean dirt.

Next, collect some sticks and break them up into 4 inch lengths. I like to have 8 of them ready, four with bark on and four bare. If you elect to 'go barked', make sure that the bark is still on tight to the stick. It's bothersome when it comes off prematurely. I like having the first four sticks barked, and the last four 'flagged'. If you take a wet-wipe and tear it lengthwise into four pieces, the pieces will be the perfect width to wrap the ends of your sticks with. Wrap these up so they look like tootsie pops and have them ready. I like having them all lined up for use from left to right.

Now, down with your shorts, squat down, and lean against the tree you're with your rear centered over the hole. You shouldn't be completely square against the tree, but should have one cheek harder against it than the other. This helps 'get the bomb bay doors' more open so to speak.

Now take a small pebble or stick, hold it directly under your third eye and drop it. Observe where it goes. If it's in the hole, you're free to go. If it missed the hole or landed in your shorts, you may want to reposition before embarking on the main event.

When it's clean-up time start with the barked spudgers first. Only use one end, they're disposable and drop each one into the hole after use. The flagged sticks take a little more finesse. These need to be used with a twirling motion, and twirled only in the direction that serves to tighten the flags further. Spin them the wrong way, and the soiled flags fall off onto your hand.

When you're done, you should be able to wave a used little white flag before you drop it into the hole. If the last flag isn't completely white, break more sticks and make more flags. When you're all done, use a bigger stick to cover the hole and tamp it down. I like to leave that stick on top and sort of leaning against the tree in a little bit of an unnatural position. This signals to the alert hiker that 'this tree has been fed' and to take his trowel elsewhere. After all that, use the hand sanitizer and stow everything away.

Most people don't follow this protocol I suspect, so I never under any circumstances share or accept trail mix from other hikers. Who knows what's under their fingernails? The only person I'll share food with in the woods is my son Matthew, a fellow adherent to the protocol. There's plenty of stuff under his fingernails too, don't get me wrong. But the stuff under his fingernails isn't that stuff, if you know what I mean.

Once I was finished with all that, and everything stowed back in my pack, I decided to wait for Sheila while taking a nap. Not because I was really tired but because my feet were hurting. Besides, it was cool in the shade. I woke later to stomping footsteps. It was Sheila.

"This is just like home here," I said.

"I don't care, did you get water?"

"Yeah, it's about a quarter mile behind you."

"WHAT? Why didn't you stop there?"

"You know? We shouldn't hike together. You're not a morning person, you're grouchy at night, and here we are conversing at midday and you're being a butt," I said.

"What's a butt?"

"I think the Australian term may be A-hole."

That was the last conversation we had. Occasionally I'd hear stories about Sheila from incredulous hikers on the trail from time to time, like how she'd scolded a barista about the correct way to present espresso and how she once browbeat a young couple into sharing their room with her at a hotel.

At the next camp a fast and efficient looking guy came in. He got out his stove and made himself dinner in a matter of minutes. "There was a lady back there that told me to get her water. Why would she do that?", he asked.

"Meet all kinds here, I guess."

"Naw, PCT'ers are pretty good," he said. "I did the Appalachian Trail last year and some of those people are terrible. On the AT, you're supposed to sleep in designated shelters, and when it rains people stick their butts out under the eaves to crap. Seriously. They don't want to get wet on their way to the outhouse." He savored his noodles a minute. "I hated it you know? Swore I'd never through hike again. But then I was reading about how the PCT had a new permit system and for some reason I thought 'Well, I better get one'. So now here I am."

He finished his noodles, swung on his pack and left. He said he liked to hike another five or ten miles after dinner every night before setting up camp. "Bonus miles," he called them.

The next night's camp I had picked out while planning the hike last winter wasn't as cool in person as it looked from Google Earth images. It was only six more miles to the highway to Big Bear so I kept walking.

At the highway was a cooler full of ice and cream soda. It was delicious. I was just about to hit 'confirm' on the uber app when a white minivan pulled over and parked. A middle-aged man with gold rimmed glasses and a crewcut got out. "Any of you guys need a ride into town? I'm going for a short walk and when I get back I'll take you."

There were four of us there but only two of us were going in to town, myself and ponytailed guy that talked only about mushrooms. "It's the mycelium, I'm telling you it's the earth's internet. If only all of us humans ate more mushrooms telepathy would be within our grasp."

"Really?" I asked. "What am I thinking right now?"

He looked at me. "You don't eat mushrooms like I do," he said.

"Whoa! You ARE telepathic!" I told him.

The minivan guy came back. "My name is Norm. Who's going?"

It was a seven-mile ride into town and Norm gave me and the mushroom kid some local history. Half of the seats were out of the minivan, a perfect configuration for hauling hikers with large backpacks. I asked Norm why he gave PCT hikers rides into town.

"Well I didn't always," Norm said. "But a couple years ago my mother passed away on a Mother's Day weekend. I didn't want to see anyone, or talk to anyone, or even to do anything with anyone really. I grew up in Acton and the PCT goes through there and when I was a kid I'd see hikers going through. So I thought, 'the PCT is just up the road. I'll just go up there for a walk by myself'."

"And when I got there," he said, "there were a couple of dirty and tired hikers that asked me for a ride to town. So I put off my walk and drove them. But when I got back to the trailhead for my hike, there were more hikers that wanted to get to town. I never got to walk that day, all day long I kept shuttling hikers into town. And you know what, that kind of got me out of that funk, doing something useful. So from then on every evening I come up here for a stroll and see if anyone needs a ride into town. And you know what else?" he asked. "I never accept gas money or payment of any kind. I only require that my riders help a stranger somehow within the next two months."

There was silence a moment while the mushroom and I digested Norm's story.

"Well shoot, Norm," I said. "You coulda' told us that before we got in, you know."

Norm took his eyes off the road a second to look at me. "Ha! I've got you," he said. "And when you do that kindness, and I know you will, tell them that 'Norm made me do it', you hear?"

DJ AND TONI

Miles on Trail... 191

This is why I'm not a real traveler- whenever I get to a place I kind of like, I start thinking about how to live there. Big Bear was like that. It's a ski resort town with a big lake complete with marina, and has great hiking and ORV trails. If they couldn't use a GIS analyst, I was thinking maybe I could rent out jeeps or water skis.

However I found a way to stay there, I'd eat dinner at Gaby's every night I could. Gaby is Bolivian, her husband Javier is Mexican and they have a restaurant in an older house on Big Bear's main drag. They live upstairs, but even when you're downstairs in the restaurant you feel more like a family friend than a customer. "With Mexican food you need to add pico de gallo or tamale sauce to being out the flavor," Javier told me. "Bolivian food comes out of the kitchen ready to go. And Gaby is the best." He's right.

I spent two nights in Big Bear resupplying my food bag, treating my blistered feet, and buying new shoes, which had somehow shrunk while walking through the desert. Actually it was my feet that had changed. I had hiked 93 miles in the first 5 days on the trail, and my feet had grown two and a half sizes, from 10 ½ to size 13.

A little about blisters...Your feet are probably too small. I read somewhere that the average American walks about 2 miles per month. Health experts and virtually everyone else agree this is not enough. One weird consequence of not walking enough is that your feet begin to shrink. All the muscles, tendons, and connective tissue that make up your feet and hold the bones of your foot together begin to atrophy and as a consequence shrink to the size dictated by the level of your activity, or inactivity as the case may be. In my younger years as a dairy farmer and later as a mountain climber I was on my feet almost continuously every waking hour. At that time, I wore a size 13 shoe. But in the years since I had slowed down, gotten myself a cushy office job, and didn't walk as far as I used to or even spend all that much time standing up. My feet shrank two and a half sizes.

I started my hike wearing a good pair of size 10 and half shoes, that fit my feet perfectly. I started getting blisters on the bottoms of my feet and on the back of my heels after my second day of hiking while coming down Fuller Ridge in the heat and the wind storm. Not long after I noticed that my shoes seem to be getting too small. I assumed that my feet were swollen because of the blistering on the backs of my heels. I developed full blisters on the bottoms of all my toes and the bottom of the balls of both feet. It was like walking on two fluid-filled bags attached to the bottoms of my feet. For the next hundred and ten miles to the next town I had to walk balanced on little waterbeds and with my toes curled up.

When I got to Big Bear I went to a shoe store for a new pair of shoes and was surprised to find that in one week of hiking my feet had grown two and a half sizes, from 10 1/2 to 13. My blisters had popped by then so the extra volume that my feet took up was all feet, not the miniature waterbeds that had been on my soles. I was back to the size shoe I wore in my prime, so I was happy to have them on my feet again. I wore size 13 on my feet for the next 2400 miles and never had a problem.

Your skin is like a quilt, with layers. A quilt has a top layer, a bottom layer, and batting in between. The layers are held together with stitching. Your skin is sort of constructed similarly. You get blisters when you are doing something that breaks the "stitching" that holds the layers of your skin together. When the shear force between your skin's layers becomes too great, the tissue connecting the layers of your skin tear and the interstitial space is filled with serous fluid. You have a blister.

You generate a lot of shear forces as you walk. Your foot and all its internal architecture is forced forwards, backwards, downwards, upwards with each step. Your foot flexes, bends, and changes shape constantly as you move over the ground. It's tough for your skin to keep up. I remember wearing hand-me-down rubber boots a couple sizes too big when I was a kid. My socks always slipped off my feet and ended up as a wad in the toes of the boots after running or galumping around in those boots. The friction of the sock-to-boot interface was greater than the sock-to-skin interface. The interface with the least resistance failed, a slip plane was created between my socks and my feet, and the boots were able to strip the socks off my feet.

The trick to preventing blisters is to control the location of the slip planes. You'll want to keep the slip planes outside your body as much as possible. Shoe tread to ground, sock to shoe lining, skin to sock. Out there. Allowing the slip plane to develop inside your body, epidermis to dermis, will cause blistering.

Make sure our shoes fit. Do what you can to keep your feet dry- sweat increases the friction of everything inside your shoe. Use duct tape or moleskin on your feet to make them more slippery. Wear socks with slippery material that shears. Develop a good set of callouses.

Calloused skin is fantastic. On the outside, the skin is tough and slick. On the inside, the connective tissue is incredibly strengthened. It's the body's method of controlling the location of the slip plane, evicting to the outside. When blisters heal, they become callouses. So don't worry too much if your choice of shoes or socks wasn't so good, or your conditioning was lacking and you give yourself blisters. Your body will make callouses out of them.

Getting out of Big Bear and back on the trail wasn't as easy as getting in. Which was ok I guess because it made me quit thinking about moving the family there. If you ever think you may be unduly enamored with a new town, you should try out their public transport. Everyone on the bus was coughing and phlegmy, wearing a walking boot, or couldn't fit into the seats provided. An emaciated and nicotine-stained toothless codger turned around in his seat to complain about how much of a busybody rumor mill the town was.

"Lemme give ya an example," he told me. "Last year my boy up and had enough and so shoots hisself dead. So's the police come and tells me about it cause I'm next of kin and his mother don't live here anymores. And you know what? When I sobered up and went in to Rite Aid the lady at the counter had herself a heart attack 'cause she'd heard I was the one that done it. What do you think of that, hey?"

"That's awful", I said.

"Damned right it is," he said. "People should mind their own business."

"Well," I said, "I've always tried."

The bus got me to the post office, I got my stuff, mailed my now-too-small shoes back home and then hit the road. I figured on hitchhiking back to the trailhead and making another 11 trail miles but it became clear that this wasn't happening. The highway back to the trailhead had narrow shoulders and wasn't very conducive to hitchhiking. There just wasn't any real place for a driver to pull over. Cars flew past my elbow at 65. If I had stuck my thumb out, someone would have taken my hand off.

I got off the shoulder and looked at a map. Crossing through a couple backyards and a gravel pit and some cross-country hiking would lead to an off-road jeep trail that eventually intersected the main trail. I figured it would be easier to avoid stepping on a rattlesnake out there than becoming a messy hood ornament down here. So that was it for hitchhiking.

It was about an hour trespassing through backyards and the gravel pit to the steep open timber beyond. My backpack started ringing. The GPS unit I carry also acts as a tracker, so friends and family back home can send text messages and follow my progress online.

"You are 4 miles west of the trail, turn right," said one text.

"Looks like bear dragging your pack up mountain. Text back if true," said another. I couldn't think of a reasonable scenario where I could comply with that directive, but it was heartwarming knowing that people back home cared for me.

The jeep road was awesome. In some places all of the gravel had been clawed off and the bare bedrock had been clambered over and polished smooth by rubber tires. The only people crazier than the folks driving over this stuff had to be the ones renting them the vehicles to do it with.

The views looking down to Big Bear Lake from the jeep road were nice, but all the goofing off trying to hitchhike out of town and the cross country travel put me behind schedule. The elevation was high enough that it got cold when the sun slipped below the horizon so I had to stop for the night a couple miles short of my target. It wasn't a bad spot, and there was already a tent set up nearby though I never saw anyone outside of it.

That night my water bottles froze inside my tent and I learned that my lightweight sleeping bag wasn't really sufficient. I had to wear all my clothes, including raingear, and burned all of my cooking fuel making hot water bottles to get through the night with. In the morning, I packed up wearing socks on my hands. I still didn't see or hear anyone from the other tent.

So far I'd seen a lot of people out here without much in the way of experience or resourcefulness, and I began to worry. Did that guy just freeze to death next to me last night? I called through the tent fabric and was answered by two startled voices—one deep, gruff, and angry; the other higher-pitched, and confused. But neither of them sounded cold or lonesome, or appreciative of any offer for help.

I never saw anyone that day either, and hiked most of the day through a burned out forest turned desert. When the climate is that dry and that close to the edge it's impossible for a burned forest to recover and the desert plants take over. Cactus growing in ashes.

Not far off the trail at the end of the day there was a copse of mature pine trees that had escaped the fire so I made camp there. It was a wonderful spot, and before the fire must have been a popular campsite in the area. It had a couple abandoned grilled firepits and a sign that said in Big block letters 'YOU ARE HERE', but the map below had faded and weathered away. I liked that sign. People at work think I hate signs, but I'm actually a connoisseur of sorts and I only tear down signs around the office of craven jackassery like 'Your Mother Doesn't Work Here!' and their ilk. But this one- 'YOU ARE HERE' over a big blank space struck me as an existential affirmation of sorts. Comforting if you think about it.

It reminded me of the time when Monica was trying to get Matthew to remember and recite a nightly creed at bedtime. He was only three at the time, and making rough work of it so Monica asked me to rework the creed into something more compact that a three year-old could remember and understand while still retaining the creed's basic message. So the version I taught Matthew to recite was this:

> The world is bigger than we think it is.
> We are a part of it.
> And nobody wants to see my wiener.

As far as living within a healthy worldview goes, I still think it's better than most.

The next morning I saw that someone had put signs on the trail, like the sandwich boards signs used for real estate open houses. They said that there would be free hamburgers at Splinter Cabin on Saturday. Hey. I got my phone out and checked. Today was Saturday and Splinter Cabin was just eight miles ahead. It may have perked up my pace a bit, but not as much as the guy coming up behind me. I stepped off to let him pass. He was youngish, probably a just few years north of thirty, short hair and a neatly trimmed beard. He was squinting and walking with his head down. He had a large bandana tied to the back of his pack. The top part of it, where it was tied had a nice paisley pattern. The bottom part of it was an indiscriminate greasy mass. By flicking his shoulders he could swing the grimy end within reach so he could jam it into his eye.

"Stupid bug just flew straight into my eyeball," he said. "Now he's crawling around in there, driving me nuts."

Even with one eye, the guy was faster than me so I wished him a good day and said I hoped to see him at Splinter's.

"Naw, at this rate I'll get there too early. And besides, I feel like talking. Last night was the worst I had since I got on the trail and it helps to talk about it. I'm DJ, by the way," he said.

He got behind me again and continued. "I get these nightmares see, I've been having them since I was a kid. I grew up in crack houses and my parents were addicts and you just never knew who would be in the house, or when they might show up, or what they'd do when they got there, see? So it would be hard to sleep, and then when I did get to sleep I'd have these nightmares about big faceless guys chasing me and trying to kill me and stuff. I'd run, but always too slow and then I'd wake up with my heart pounding and all agitated up, you know? And whenever that happened, that feeling would just stick with me all day.

"When I was fifteen, my older sister got out and took me with her so we left Portland and went north to a little town called Burlington. That summer I picked berries and made some money and bought the brightest colored clothes I could find. It was the 90s right? Everyone on MTV was wearing bright stuff and I wanted to fit in with kids at the new school. So then the night before school's first day, my sister is giving me a haircut and the little plastic guard falls off and she cuts a stripe all the way down to my skull. So then the only thing to do was to finish off the rest of it to match. I stuck out like a sore thumb there 'cause all the country kids were wearing denims and baseball caps and me there with my bright clothes and skinhead head.

"And then this kid I'd never seen before in my life, he notices that I'm kind of embarrassed and shy cause I look so weird and I don't know where my next class is and he pulls the John Deere hat off his head and puts it on mine and says, 'Here you go', and just walks off.

"I was speechless, no one had ever done anything so nice for me in my whole life, and I decided right then that I'd be a country boy for the rest of my life. But I kept having those dreams and getting killed every night, so when I graduated I joined the Marines and became an expert in jiu-jitsu and hand-to-hand combat and taught myself to confront the faceless guy in my nightmares. But it didn't do me no good 'cause when I'd take the knife from the guy and stab him with it, he'd just laugh and pull out a frying pan or an Uzi or something and keep right on killing me. It sucks.

"I've been in the war and have PTSD. I also have ADHD and ADD, and I smoke all the marijuana I can afford and it helps some. I'm married now to a woman that sees good in me and we have two boys, ten and thirteen and it's pretty good. Right now I'm kind of between jobs and my license is suspended so we thought it would be a good time to go hike and get rid of these nightmares once and for all. See if I hike twenty miles and then sleep on the ground there's no nightmares, so we thought if I did that for five months straight it might be a cure. But then last night I was setting up camp and this guy straggles in looking all shot so I felt sorry for him and gave him the nice level spot I was fixing to use and set up on sloped rocky ground instead. So I'm sliding off my pad all night and the big dude with the knife came back in the nightmare to kill me again all night so I didn't get any sleep. And now this stupid bug just kamkazeed my eyeball."

We hiked along quietly for an hour or so, me taking in the scenery and DJ watching my heels and working the bug out of his eye with the greaseball end of his rag. Even at my pace, the two of us came up behind another hiker who was moving even slower.

Every once in a while the guy's left foot would come down sideways, pointing across his body at the 3 o'clock position. When this happened, his right foot would trip over it, he'd catch himself with his trekking poles, and stop a second to pull his left foot up to his rear- like he was trying to kick himself in the butt - and then continue on hiking. His trail name was Mr. Calamity. DJ had gotten his bug out by this time and was feeling a little more cheerful, so asked Mr. Calamity about his crazy foot.

"Well, a couple years ago I was reloading my Glock and it has clips that you shove into the bottom of the grip. I was pushing in a new clip with my right hand with my left hand on top, but the palm of my hand was on the hammer and the safety was off. So when I pushed in the new clip, my hand slipped and the gun went off- shot myself point blank through my left knee. It split my femur and totally destroyed my inner condoyle. You know how the bottom of your femur is supposed to have these two bumps on it where your knee is? Well, one of those got blown off so I only have one of them. It took a couple surgeries and 8 weeks of no walking, but it works pretty good now as long as I'm not in too much of a hurry and I have hiking sticks with me."

He and DJ talked handguns for a while, their favorite brands, ammunition and other technicalities. I was curious only about one thing, so I asked Mr. Calamity why he had purchased a gun in the first place.

"Well," he said, "I was living in Arizona."

"Exactly!" said DJ.

Exactly what, I have no idea and probably never will.

The Desert Mountain Walkers Club had a big spread of potluck style food and picnic tables set up when we got to Splinter Cabin, and signs congratulating hikers for making 300 miles. There was already a sizeable group of hikers there, many of which had camped there the night before. I was pleased to meet another hiker there close to my age. He said his name was Gary.

"Gary? Is that your regular name or your trail name, like Gary on Spongebob?," asked DJ.

"Who's Spongebob?"

"Spongebob is the greatest kids show ever, he's a sponge and he has a pet named Gary. Gary is a snail," said DJ.

"Gary is a snail? Then that's my trail name," said Gary.

I sampled some home-made cookies, chatted with some of the event hosts and took a seat at a picnic table just downwind of the grilling hamburgers. There's something about the smell of meat cooking over fire that enters a man's nose and goes straight to the ancient part of his brain. It's a primal thing, it makes me feel somehow triumphant, confident- masterful and satisfied. I don't know how or why, but I like it.

So I just sat there with my eyes closed, feeling the sun and smelling the smoke when a sweet voice said "Hi, I'm Toni. Mom said you like my cookies. Mind if I sit here?"

It's tough to improve upon the aroma of grilling meat, but Toni did. Intermingled now with the grilling smoke, came the smells of cheap shampoo, enthusiasm and youth. Toni was a beauty in her mid-twenties, dark hair past her shoulders, perfectly tanned skin, and a cute smallish nose. She was easy enough to listen to as she chatted along in a sort of air-heady way.

"Mom and Dad have been members of this hiking club for, oh I don't know, forever you know. I only go to some of these events. That's them sitting right over there."

Across from us were a middle-aged couple in lawn chairs watching us. I waved and they smiled back.

"Oh, I loved the PCT. You're going to love it. I met a guy at this event last year and we did twelve hundred miles before we got stopped by the fires."

"Did you hitch around the fires to carry on?" I asked.

"No, after the fires stopped us we kind of lost momentum and just kind of quit, you know? But it was a good long run."

As Toni chatted along with Gary, I started wondering- how does a person just decide to go off on a 2,000-mile trail with someone they'd just met? Not only that, but there's the logistics. I'd been dreaming of this trip my whole life and seriously planning for it for the last three years. The simple answer- you don't. It couldn't have been a spur of the moment decision.

I looked around at the other tables. There were two guys with tattooed faces over there rolling joints. Another couple guys were trying to get people to sign their 'tents'- actually irregularly shaped scraps of Tyvek with home-made duct-taped grommet holes. There were some Kiwi guys trying to woo a couple Austrian girls I thought of as the Snot-Smockers. Their septums were pierced through with barbells, and the snot dripping off them over the last couple weeks had crusted their shirts into stiff breastplates. Sure enough, Toni's parents had set up their lawn chairs to oversee the picnic table that seated the most respectable appearing hikers. Or at least, the least odd of the odd. I asked Toni what people do around here.

"Oh nothing really. Just hike trails and drink beer. That's all there is to do."

"No, that's not what I mean.", I said. "What I mean is if you got married and had babies here, what would you and your husband be doing for a living?"

"Oh, no. That can't happen here," she said looking away. I followed her gaze. Her mother was staring back at her, almost imperceptibly shaking her head 'no'. Her dad seemed to be staring at me- stony faced, assessing.

So I let the subject drop and finished off some kind of bean salad. I was willing to bet that Toni's backpack was ready to go in case she found a guy her folks approved of. In that event, I wondered if she'd have to run home to get it or if it was already in the back of her parents' truck. I looked at Toni's shoes. She was wearing Altra's, a specialized type of trail shoe that's reported to be the ultimate PCT trail shoe. The backpack was probably in the truck.

As I left, I walked over to Toni's folks and thanked them for the food and nice outing. I told them that my family was home at the other end of the trail and that I still had a long ways to go to get back to them. Toni's dad, who hadn't said a word the entire morning, stuck his hand out.

As I shook it, he said, "I completely understand. Be safe."

I wonder if Toni will make it out of town and onto the trail this year; if she does, I hope she can make a good, long run of it.

"Be prepared for nudity," Toni had warned. "You're going to see a lot of naked people in the next ten miles," she said. "Try to keep your eyes up here."

"To heck with that," I thought. "If naked people show up, I'm going to check them out all over. Why else would they be naked?"

There's no practical reason to walk around naked, and really the only reason nudists do it is to prove to themselves and others how special they are. "See how I'm doing something that most people won't. I'm Special." Yeah, I know that's not what nudists say. I have a nudist friend and I've heard the 'freedom and body image' spiel. It's all crap. They just want to feel special, but really it's just a cheap trick. If they really want to be special, they should sit behind a piano and play Chopin or something. But that's too difficult so they take their clothes off instead.

Near Deep Creek a group of them came up the trail towards me, just as Toni had warned. They were middle aged and two of each gender and were happy to stop in the trail and chat about the weather. I took the opportunity to inspect them thoroughly up and down. All of them were wearing sun hats and sandals, and carrying water bottles rolled up in beach towels. The guys had beards and glasses, and looked pleased with themselves. The women looked tired or maybe dumb and wore vacant parade float smiles on their faces.

On the guys, there was more hair than you'd think necessary between their hats and their sandals. The parts with the least hair hung like wrinkled, useless turkey snoods. They weren't sunburned, but were coated with trail dust grimed onto what I think was zinc oxide. They looked- well they looked ridiculous.

For the women, there were fewer details of note. They looked kind of sad and saggy. Parts of them were unappetizingly coated with trail dust and zinc oxide as well.

One of the naked dudes was telling me exactly how many miles I had to go to get to Canada and how it would be such a spiritual journey. As we passed I told him:

"The world is bigger than we think it is. We are a part of it."

"That is so true!"naked dude said.

"And nobody wants to see your weiner," I finished.

ART AND BUCKWHEAT

Miles on Trail... 274

The trail, after it leaves Deep Creek, winds three quarters of the way around Silverwood Lake, a reservoir that artificially receives several watersheds to help feed Los Angeles. I had planned to camp on one of the beaches there, but was a little ahead of schedule. So I passed by the beaches and went instead to a boat-in picnic area at Chamois Point. It was Sunday afternoon, and the garbage cans were overflowing with the weekend's crowds that had already left. Other than the flies, I had the place to myself. I sat at a covered table with my head on my arms and took a nap.

A 60-year old speedboat like the kind you saw in the sixties beach movies was coming to the point. Crowded into the boat around a twin-piped V-8 engine with no protective cowling was an Hispanic family of six. A young guy was driving, his young wife, three kids (one a baby), and a slightly tipsy father-in-law made up his crew. The boat had only a couple inches of freeboard.

"Hey Papi!,"he yelled. "When I get close I'm gonna cut the f'ing engine. You hop off with the f'ing rope and pull us the rest of the way in so we don't scrape our f'ing bottom, 'kay?"

Papi found the rope and tiptoed awkwardly around kids, hot engine manifolds, loose picnic coolers, and over the windshield onto the bow. When the motor was cut, he toppled over the front and into the water. The boat caught the dead swell from behind and rolled up on top of him.

"What the f_ you doin', Papi!", yelled the captain. "you dropped the f'ing rope!"

The captain had to take matters into his own hands to keep from scraping onto the rocks. So he jumped out but as he did, caught his sandal on a cleat and went in headfirst. He hung there upside down for a bit like one of those guys in the cowboy movies that get shot off a galloping horse, and get dragged along with a foot stuck in a stirrup. As his head hit bottom in the shoal water, the boat slewed sideways and skidded over him. His foot came loose as he keel-hauled himself and he popped up on the other side. His sandal stayed in the boat.

After a little wrangling, Papi and the captain got the boat tied up and anchored a little offshore so the rocks wouldn't scratch up the ancient fiberglass. They took their shirts off to dry out a bit. Papi had a giant prison tattoo across his back that said PLANO. He was a big guy.

It was interesting how they talked with each other, there was sort of a hierarchy about it. The captain f'd this and f'd that to everyone else in the family. He didn't sound mean or mad or anything, it was just the way he talked. No one took any notice. Papi peppered his language with f-bombs only when he talked with the Captain. He didn't sound angry either, but never f-bombed his daughter or grandkids. That was for the Captain only. Mom and the kids didn't f-bomb anyone. As they got the picnic underway there were other differences. The two men were served first, and only the men had Coke from cans. Mom and the kids drank Sprite from paper cups.

I needed to refill my water bottles and as I came down to their beach the Captain eyed me suspiciously. It was tense, he was a proud young Hispanic man with his family and I was a white middle-aged man of vaguely Aryan descent that had just witnessed his humiliating boat handling skills. But as I got closer his eyes widened, and his expression softened because I looked- well I looked pretty pathetic.

You can't shower when you've been walking through deserts and ash fields for four days. And it doesn't do any good to wash your clothes when wind is blowing dirt all over all the time either. I had lost sixteen pounds since I started walking and my pants kept falling off. When I used a belt to cinch them up, I got blisters under my backpack where the waistband bunched up. The day before, I'd hit on the idea of carabinering the two front belt loops together to bunch all the slack in my trousers to the front. No backpack chafing, but it made me look like Charlie Chaplin- only dirtier.

"Man, are you like, walking to Canada?" asked the Captain. Canada. Not f'ing Canada. I wasn't sure what this meant.

"Yeah, I'm trying to," I said. "Hey," I said dipping water from the lake," There's no sheen behind this boat."

"What?"

"No sheen. Most boats have a little oil sheen behind them. This one doesn't."

"Yeah man, I rebuilt that engine myself," said the Captain. "Top to bottom. It's tight."

We talked about the boat for a while as his kids ran around the beach collecting rocks. It was nice.

As I got ready to go, he said, "Hey man. Would you like a soda or something?"

" You know I got nothing to trade for it."

"Yeah, yeah I know but take this." He handed me a roll of Ritz crackers. "Mama, get something out of the cooler."

"I'll get him some Sprite," his wife said.

"No, no. Give the man a f'ing Coke." Then to me, he said, "My name's Art. What's yours?"

That evening, eight or ten miles north I saw my family with Duo and had a delicious meal of Ritz crackers with cheese. Monica had just broken her arm the day before and her sister and niece were there to get her settled at home. On the screen, I could see kids and family and a fire going in the woodstove. She looked beautiful and loved, even though I wasn't there with her. Percocet was making her nose itch, so every once in a while a gauzed and cobanned sock puppet would come up from the bottom of the screen to scratch her nose with purplish fingertips peeking out from the bandaging. She ate pizza while I finished my Ritz and cheese, I talked a little with everyone in the house. I wasn't home, but my family was - and I was still part of it.

I felt satisfied. That night, thoughts drifted from my family to Art's, and I tried to imagine what they might be doing. After fighting traffic with a boat trailer back to east LA, Art probably washed and put everything away while his family ate and watched TV. I imagined him eating dinner late by himself at the kitchen table while his wife herded the kids to bed. Tomorrow would probably see him at the jobsite early for a long day of doing something unpleasantly difficult but essential. I didn't know what. Really, I didn't know anything about Art's life.

All I knew for sure was that Ritz makes a good f'ing cracker.

Cajon Pass was a dry desolate place. It had a six-lane freeway going through and several railroad tracks. Nobody lives there. There were a couple old houses that have been burned out, and a small cemetery from years past. The cemetery had most of its headstones knocked over. Wind whistled around rusting hulks of old vehicles and kitchen appliances with bullet holes in them. In their midst was a small bronze monument commemorating the area's listing on the National Registry of Historical Sites. The newer parts of Cajon Pass consisted mainly of a six-lane freeway, railroad tracks, a McDonald's, and a Best Western on a freeway frontage road. As I walked up the frontage road to the McDonald's I passed a parked 18-wheeler. The refrigeration unit on the trailer was running, but I didn't see the driver. Maybe he was in the sleeper compartment. On the gravel shoulder next to the parked truck was a makeshift tent, partially shredded by the wind and shorn up with blue tarp and old shopping carts with tumbleweeds stuck in them. Just outside the tent's entrance was a worn and sun-bleached wheelchair.

I couldn't help but wonder what shape someone's life's road would lead to that tent in the wind in the desert beside an interstate on a trucking route. It was a sad and disturbing scene to contemplate, so I decided to quit that and to think about fast food instead.

When I got to the McDonald's it was too early for the lunchtime menu, so I ordered myself a couple of McGriddles and a large coffee. It was all sticky and delicious. I had a shave in the bathroom and left well satisfied and clean-looking. As I left McDonald's and headed back to the trail, I came across Buckwheat. He had spent the night in the Best Western hotel next to the McDonald's to visit his wife. We walked a bit at his pace and chatted, and then I moved ahead on my own. As the trail wound its way up the grassy foothills and out of the pass, the wind became stronger and stronger. I experimented by leaning into the wind with my backpack at different angles of attack. The wind was strong enough that when I had the correct position the wind could lift my backpack up to take the weight off my shoulder straps and hip belt. If the wind would have remained constant it would have been great, but the wind was erratic and strong gusts would push me off balance.   To keep from being pushed off the trail and over a cliff I would drop to hands and knees. Once, I startled a rattlesnake.

I began to worry about Buckwheat behind me. He's a short slight man and I knew that he would likely be having more trouble with the wind than me. I found a sheltered spot just off the trail to wait for him. When Buckwheat caught up, I slowed my pace to match his. The trail topped out at a ridge that had once been lightly timbered, but had been used as a fire break the year before. There were excavator tracks and big holes where they had dug trees out by the roots as part of the fire break. The wind was still howling. I walked through the ashes to crouch down in one of the tree holes that had been excavated out.

"Buckwheat," I called. "The wind isn't too bad down in these holes. I think we should pick foxholes for ourselves to set up tents for the night."

"No way," said Buckwheat. "My phone app doesn't say there's a campsite here. The next campsite is two miles ahead."

"I know that," I said, looking at the map on his phone screen. "See, look at where that camp is on the topo. The wind at the next campsite is going to be even worse than it is right here."

"But the phone doesn't say that this is a camp right here," said Buckwheat. "I won't camp here."

I thought about leaving Buckwheat to go on up the trail to the next camp by himself, but then I remembered getting that free ride from Norm into the last town. I owed a good deed to a stranger, so I said "Lead on and I'll follow. Norm told me to."

It took us another hour and a half to make the two miles to where the phone app said the next camp was. It was a small spot of dirt in the midst of sticker bushes on a steep slope. There was only room for one tent- the one that was already there. Buckwheat yelled through the fabric to the tent's occupant, "Hey move your tent just a little bit over so there's room for me to put mine too! It's windy out here!"

It was too late to push on or to go back to the ridge with the fire break, so I looked around for a desperate campsite. I found a spot just down slope of Buckwheat and the other tent, too small for me to set up my tent in. So I broke branches off sticker bushes with my bare hands. I didn't carry a machete with me in my backpack. I got my tent setup in a lumpy and uneven spot, made myself dinner with bloodied hands, and settled in for an uncomfortable night. When the wind wasn't howling, I could hear Buckwheat talking to the occupant of the other tent, who turned out to be a young man who had just finished his PhD in mathematics.

"Puzzles, you said your name is?", said Buckwheat. "Well Puzzles, my name is Buckwheat and I'm a framer. I build houses. I never had the patience to keep fooling away in college long enough to get a degree like you did. Oh, I could have if I wanted to, you know. I'm tested out as a true genius. I took lots of tests. I could even write books if I wanted to except that I have dyslexia so it's a pain in the butt for me to read or write. What brings you to the trail?"

Puzzles' voice didn't carry above the wind, and all I could hear were faint murmurings in reply.

"Oh that's a great reason to hike the trail I guess," said Buckwheat. "I'm hiking the trail because I am 66 years old, and life is just too short to put big things off. My wife was just diagnosed with breast cancer and is currently undergoing chemotherapy. See what I mean? Life's too short to put things off."

Again, I could hear murmuring replies, but I couldn't make words out over the wind. But the tone sounded as if Puzzles was a little, well puzzled.

"Well sure, why not?" asked Buckwheat. "The chemo makes her tired and so she just hangs around sleeping most of the time anyway, you know?"

I wriggled inside my tent to get back up the slope and onto my sleeping pad. As the wind pushed the tent fabric down in my face, a thought came to me. "Norm should quit giving people rides," I thought.

COOL BREEZE AND FINN

Miles on Trail... 385

The next Duo call home started with a brief glimpse of Monica in the kitchen, arm in a sling and chopping vegetables one-handed. Then the screen gyrated around wildly, showing lights, walls, and floors, finally settling on a view of the hallway as the phone was propped up on the baseboard. A bare butt came into view.

"Hi, Dad. How are you?" The butt had little hands on each side to move its cheeks as it talked. The effect was pretty good, obviously practiced.

"I'm good. Where's Judah?" The two of them were usually joined at the hip, so I half expected two of them.

"He couldn't come over today," the butt said. "He had to do something at home."

"Okay. So what's going on at school with you?"

"Well, all next week we have tests every day for assessments or whatever's and they're going to be really hard," the butt said.

"Well, just take your time and answer as many questions as you can," I said, "and you'll be fine. I can tell I'm speaking with an intelligent young man."

"Uh huh." The butt decided that now was a good time to spank its cheeks red. "I'm not worried."

"Good. How about you go wash your hands and then give the phone to your mom?"

"Okay." The butt slid out of view; had an idea, and came back on screen. "Hey, Dad," it said. "You want to see how I brush my teeth?"

A side trail brings you out of the mountains and into Wrightwood. Some of the houses I passed had plastic chest coolers out by the street with bottled water or pop in them. I'd camped only 10 miles away so it was early enough to get breakfast at a coffee shop. There was a coffee thermos there with a sign saying 'Free to PCT Hikers.' I got myself a cup and was scolded by the barista, "That's free for PCT hikers only," she said. "That will be a dollar fifty for you." I was pleased that my meticulous trail shaving routine was showing results and paid for the compliment. I couldn't find a place to get new pants that fit, but did get a new set of hiking sticks at the hardware store. Also, a pair of gloves. Last time it was cold enough to need them, I had to use dirty socks instead. I didn't like the way my hands smelled the rest of the day.

Getting back to the trail was a lot easier this time. Cindy, the Airbnb host, was leaving for work early and said she'd take me the seven miles to drop me off at the trailhead and insisted that it was on her way. But it wasn't. It wasn't on the way to anywhere, she'd run me out there just to be nice. When she left the parking lot, she went back down the highway the way we had come.

It was freezing and snowing lightly, dry fake looking stuff, and I was glad to have the new wool gloves. I met a guy that turned out to be a great hiking partner and we teamed up for the section. Cool Breeze was little older than me, and this was his second time doing the PCT. We had about the same pace, didn't need to talk much and we were both 'budless', a rarity on the PCT. Most of the other hikers spend the whole of their time wearing at least one earbud to pipe smartphone music to their brains all day as they hike. Both of us preferred hearing what was in the air around us.

Of course 'Cool Breeze' was his trail name, his non-hiking name was David. But Cool Breeze fit him pretty well out here. He's the kind of guy that doesn't need to say or hear a lot of words, and has the habit of just walking off abruptly if he thinks you're done talking- or if he thinks you should be done talking. A hiking companion some years back complained that he'd discovered several times that he'd been abandoned and was carrying on a conversation with nothing more than a 'Cool Breeze'.

A little about trail names. I'd had a conversation earlier with another guy doing the PCT for the second time, Bill, aka Two Shakes. He told me that he got his trail name on his earlier trip in 2004 before social media in his opinion had wrecked the whole trail name tradition. Back then, he said, trail names were semi-spiritual; they were supposed to reflect and reveal something unique about an individual that that person may not have even noticed about himself. In the older tradition you are offered a trail name by a thoughtful and observant fellow hiker, not labeled with one. Bill had hiked about 100 miles or so with a guy in 2004 when one day his partner asked why, every time he got something out of his pack, he'd shake it twice before putting it on. Bill hadn't even realized he'd been doing it. He's answered to Two Shakes ever since.

Bill said that now people are too eager to have a cool sounding trail name that they can post on Facebook. A lot of them make up their own names before they even get on a trail. "Most peoples' trail names today are about managing an online image they want to project," he said. Two Shakes thought this was sacrilegious.

There had been some guys that were calling me JR as a trailname. Whenever anyone asked my name I'd say "Just Rick," so they started calling me JR for short. I was never asked if I liked it or not, nor was it really any kind of personal observation. These guys hadn't hiked with me much and didn't know me very well. Couldn't, because they were never out of bed early enough.

So when Cool Breeze said, "Hey, I have a trail name suggestion for you to try on to see how you think it might fit for you," I was ready to listen. This name was an offering. JR was a label. "Finn," he said. "Like Huckleberry Finn. When you pack up camp everything is in your pack and you're gone quicker than Huckleberry Finn. You can try that name if you like it."

The more I thought about it, the more I liked it. Since then I've been introducing myself to the other hikers on the trail as 'Finn'.

The trail out of Wrightwood largely parallels the Angeles Crest Highway. There apparently was some kind of trail detour to protect an endangered yellow legged frog, so we were supposed to skip several miles of trail and walk along the highway instead. This struck me as kind of strange, but only because I was trying to figure it out. How many frogs were being run over by cars on the highway, I wondered, versus those saved by taking hikers off a walking path. And how many hikers would be run over on the highway detour? It was weird.

As it turned out, Cool Breeze and I were a good team getting around the detour area. I had decided to 'go paperless' for the section and to rely on my electronics. Cool Breeze had no use for electronics, but did have all the paper maps. There were a few moments of head scratching and a few wrong turns, but all in all we were relatively efficient getting through.

We walked through an ancient pine forest just after the detour when we could get off the highway shoulder and back on the trail. I stopped to stare up at a tree; it wasn't a pine. It looked for all the world like a Douglas Fir tree, thick gnarled bark covered its thick, and ramrod straight column of a trunk. The lowest branches were close to a hundred feet up off the ground, so I couldn't get a good look at its needles. We were in southern California and it looked like a tree that supposed to live in the rain forests of Washington. It had to be something else. I started rummaging around on the ground, looking for cones.

"Hey, Cool Breeze," I said. "This tree is weird. It looks just like an 800-year-old Doug Fir but it can't be here, you know? We're down here just east of Los Angeles, right? So what the heck is this thing doing here? How'd it get here? What is it?

31

This is weird, weird, weird. I'm trying to figure this out. Tell me- Why do YOU think this tree looks like a Doug Fir, hmm?"

"Because it is," Cool Breeze said as he walked past. Cool Breeze doesn't talk all that much, and some days not at all. But over the next weeks of traveling the same direction on the same trail, sometimes together, a sort of story emerged. After stints in the Navy and Peace Corps, he took his silvicultural degree to the US Forest Service. At that time and for most of his career the main focus of the Forest Service was to 'get the cut out'. The Forest Service would routinely build roads and bridges into public forests so big timber companies could be given sweet deals to shave the trees off for a lucrative overseas export market. Part of his job as a silviculturalist was to collect data and write reports proving that this activity was not only good forest management, but necessary for the public forest's sustainable health. At times this was a difficult job.

If smoke and mirrors wouldn't suffice, the data he collected would be thrown out and new data fabricated as needed. This developed a weird working environment. On the one hand, you could decide that even though you didn't agree with the Forest Service's overall policies, you could work from within to do what you could to blunt or someday, somehow change those policies. Or you could decide that the best thing to do was to entirely focus on your own advancement. Many of his coworkers took this Machiavellian approach, always on the lookout to steal credit from or sabotage each other's projects.

He stuck it out for almost 25 years. After that he worked as wooden boat builder, then specialty cabinetry, then mostly retirement in Arizona. There, he and his wife built a house together from the ground up; everything in the house was molded by their hands. But turned out that even though they had built the house together, they had been working on different projects. While he thought he had been building a home base for traveling, she had been building their final home to grow old and die in. After 36 years of marriage and only six months in the new house together, they decided to spend the rest of their lives apart.

Since leaving the house, he's done several hikes, bike tours, and other long-distance solo adventures. He's had some arthritis and knee joint problems and had them replaced. It's slowed him down some. Since he's had them replaced with new ones they've been used- he's logged over 10,000 miles of hiking and bicycling since the surgeries. This is his second time on the Pacific Crest Trail.

Acton is the next town out of Wrightwood on the PCT and I thought to stay there for a night, mostly because it was where Norm had grown up. Cool Breeze knew of another place he wanted to stay at in the next town up the trail so we decided to split up for a couple days and to meet again at the Green Valley fire station some thirty miles up the trail. To get to the Acton KOA I hiked through a dusty parking area where a couple dozen RVs were side by side in rows, each with generators and air conditioners running and pumping out even hotter air. There were a handful of listless PCT hikers sitting under cottonwood trees that were snowing fluff. The swimming pool was completely covered with it. There were several camp cabins with more listless people with nothing to do. They looked like they were wondering why they came. It was eleven in the morning, 90 degrees and smelled like petroleum. The next town, Agua Dulce, was only ten miles farther up the trail and over some hills so I continued on.

"I must be a real hiker now," I thought, amused at myself. Ten miles of hiking over hills through the heat didn't strike me as much of a problem. At home, I'd get in a car to go only one mile.

A couple miles up the hill was a cave where three women on an afternoon's trail hike had stopped in the shade for lunch. They had a backpack cooler. "Hey you," one of them called. "I brought too much beer and I don't want to carry it back. Come drink some, okay?"

This isn't the kind of thing that usually happens. But I have a picture to prove it.

Agua Dulce is the home of the famous 'Hiker Heaven', five acres of open field for tenting and outbuildings with toilets and showers. Cool Breeze told me that it was a must-stop for serious partying. So when I got into town and into cell range, I found another place to stay with Airbnb.

My host for the next couple nights was a nice lady named Diane. She's the sort of person that's overworked, but seems to like it that way. She was a rail-thin, four-foot ten-inch, 90 lb, 62-year old police academy cadet. She'd always wanted to be a cop, and figured she'd better get on with it before she got too old. So she drove to the Los Angeles police academy every day to run laps, do push-ups, shoot targets, and drive squad cars with men young enough to be her sons. "They think I'm an odd little old lady," she said. "But I'm still in it."

A day's hike out of Diane's I got a chance to watch some wildland firefighting drills at the Green Valley fire station. High School kids in the explorer program drove pickups or Honda Civics to the station, put on heavy boots, hard hats, and yellow shirts. Daryll, the station chief lined them out. First was what he called 'Pyramid physical training'. From the back yard of the station was a steep trail running a quarter mile up a 40 percent slope hill. It was steep. At the top of the trail was one of Daryll's EMTs. The boys' task was to walk up the hill to the EMT and back to the station, where they'd put on a 25 lb pack and make the round trip up the hill and back again. Then Daryll would load them up with an additional 35 lbs of firehoses, and a round trip up and back. This time the hoses came off, and back up the hill with 'just' the 25 lb pack. The last trip would shed the 25 lb pack.

"This simulates what we have to do to lay a hose line in steep terrain. Most of the boys grind it out and do their best to tolerate it," Daryll said. "Some make a few trips up and down the hill and decide that this isn't what they really want to do, and that's fine. But once in a while, you get a kid that sort of has an 'awakening'. You can see it. It's like they've discovered their purpose or something. See that guy?"

He pointed to a big kid jumping over some brush to get back down the hill even faster. He was smiling and shouting encouragement to the other guys. "Brush does not stop us!" he shouted. "Brush does not stop us!" they shouted back.

When he got back from his last turn, I asked him if he wanted to fight wildfires for a living. "Yeah," he said, "I can't see myself in an office inside or even really doing anything else."

"Does it worry your mom?" I asked.

"I don't know," he said. "Maybe a little."

"We have a guy here at the station whose mom still doesn't know he's a firefighter," Daryl said. "He told her he's a fire truck mechanic. He got injured in a fire once, and he told his mom that he unbolted a muffler and it fell on his face. Doesn't want his mom to worry."

As the kid went back up the hill to shout encouragements to his friends, Daryll told me about his first fire. He had been a landscaper doing some fire prevention work- cutting and chipping brush on steep slopes, when a firefighter told him that he should try out for wildfire training.

"So I went to this two-week training program," he said, "and just after that, I got sent out to a real fire. There was fire everywhere I looked, on the ground, in the trees, twirling in little tornadoes, smoke and yelling and radio traffic, chainsaws, and big planes making tanker dumps. And I thought to myself- 'What the heck am I doing here?' Two weeks of training or not, it seemed that running away was my best chance to survive. And I would have, but I couldn't see anyplace to run to- like I said, there was fire everywhere. So I did what I was told and tried not to look around too much.

"Somehow the fire got under control and then put out, I didn't die, and the other guys told me I did good and told me that I was a real firefighter. So I decided to stick with it and figure out what I was doing. That was twenty years ago."

Cool Breeze arrived. Down the road from the fire station is another PCT hiker hangout called La Casa de Luna, so named because it's about a month north of the trail's start. It's another stop if you're aim is to do as much of the trail as you can high. Cool Breeze and I camped out behind the fire station.

There was another Airbnb guest back at Diane's, a German engineer on holiday that was fascinated by the PCT. He had statistics committed to memory. "Fifty percent of all the hikers that start the PCT will drop out before they reach Agua Dulce," he said. "Another 20 percent will drop out in the next 250 miles to Kennedy Meadows. And only half of those leaving Kennedy Meadows will reach Canada," he told me.

It's a dismal success rate, but here's the thing. As I had been hiking along and meeting people on the trail, it seemed that a lot of them really weren't even trying to get to Canada. Some I'm pretty sure aren't even trying to get out of Southern California. There's legal weed, naked people in hot springs, cheap hostels, PCT party layovers, free food and stuff in 'hiker boxes', PCT hiker deals in towns. It's a pretty inexpensive way to live if you've nothing to do. And there's the Trail Angels.

Trail Angels are local folks that think of PCT hikers are pilgrims on a difficult and spiritual quest. They give PCT hikers rides, water, free food, and encouragement. They believe PCT hikers are doing something epic, inspiring, or somehow useful. Many of the PCT hikers believe the same.

And because they think they're doing something epic some of the hikers come to believe that they are entitled to whatever free stuff they can get. It's weird. And wrong. Walking 2,600 miles isn't difficult, special, rare, or especially epic. What it is, is fun, self-centered, pointless and useless. It's a long vacation. After a month of dinking along at it, I didn't really know why people think it's anything more.

And then there's a bunch of hikers that aren't really even hiking. The southern part of the trail is plentiful with cheap or free food, places to shower or set up camp, parties, and pot. And there are Trail Angels telling you how awesome you are. So they stretch it out, a cheap way to live.

These 'non-hiking' hikers are always eager for more company. "Weather forecast isn't very good for next week, might think about taking a zero." A 'zero' is trail slang for a day spent in one place going nowhere.

Clem was one of these non-hikers. We met him in 'Hikertown', where the PCT crosses a highway in the middle of nowhere. Hikertown had free water and showers, five dollar a night camping, or ten dollar beds in little toolsheds spread around the property. In the middle of it was a garage with a sofa and easy chairs salvaged from the side of the road, and a partially restored old car. Cool Breeze had been through four years earlier and seen the same car in the same condition. Progress was slow. Clem was working through his second six pack when we got there before noon. "Had to take a couple zeroes here to fix a leak in my air pad," he said. Clem spoke in an exaggerated southern drawl, wore a tattered T-shirt, bright gym shorts, and flip-flops. His toenails were painted with rainbow colors.

"Today and tomorrow are going to be hot, hot, hot across the desert section. And the next section has the trail climbing up a slope that's south facing. Going up a south facing slope is going to be hot, hot, hot. Terrible stuff," he said, getting back to his beer. "Ya might think about staying here till it cools off a bit, you know?"

That was dumb. Walking through the desert was easy enough. Carry water and leave early before it's hot. And of course you'd walk up a south-facing slope. We're walking north. If you walk DOWN a south facing slope, you're walking south.

"That foot looks like it might get infected," Clem told a twenty-something year old kid. "I'd take another day off it if'n I was you."

I asked Clem if he was leaving Hikertown that evening when the sun cooled off a bit.

"Well I ought to probably," he said, frowning. Then went back to his beer. He wasn't going anywhere.

From Hikertown the PCT crosses 31 miles of desert called the Antelope Valley before heading back into the next set of mountains, the Tehachapi range. A lot of the desert crossing follows the Los Angeles aqueduct. We left Clem at Hikertown about four in the afternoon and a couple hours later ran across Ernesto, a real life sheepherder.

Three sheepdogs barked and circled me with their hackles up, but a whistle and shouted command snapped them back to Ernesto's side. They stayed there stiffly at attention until the moment Ernesto and I shook hands; then they lost all composure. I was jumped on, licked, nuzzled. One of them wormed her way between my legs and rolled onto her back for a belly rub. Ernesto had charge of 1,500 sheep. He'd been moving them across the valley a half mile a day for the past several months. He pointed to where he was going tomorrow, and the day after, and the day after that.

Each day, another worker would come out to fetch the water truck- an ancient and rusty farm dump truck fitted with a plastic water tank and troughs, from the previous day's site and bring it filled with water to Ernesto's new location. Water out here was scarce.

There are several strategies PCT hikers use to provide themselves with safe drinking water on the trail. There are a variety of chemical treatments, miniature UV equipment, and filters. Filters seem to be the most popular. Almost everyone I've seen filtering their water out here uses a charcoal filtering system called the Sawyer Squeeze.

When I was researching the trail last winter, I came across an article that had a survey of past PCT hikers that dealt with water treatments. The only respondents that reported getting sick on the trail were those using a filter system. No one else reported getting sick, not even those that didn't treat their water at all. It's strange, but it makes sense if you think about it.

Filters work by trapping the waterborne bacteria and contaminants inside the filter cartridge as the raw water passes through. Clean drinking water comes out the other end. So far, so good. But what happens to the trapped bacteria and contaminants? Well, they stay in the filter to fester and multiply as the hiker carries the filter along. At each water stop, as the hiker uses his filter, he adds more bacteria and contaminants to the load he's already been carrying along in his filter cartridge.

This is okay as long as the cartridge keeps its load trapped. But every once in a while, something happens. The filter is dropped, stepped on, crushed in the backpack, something- something that cracks the filter matrix. On the filter's next use all the poisons, the accumulated bacteria and their by-products, flush out of the filter and into the hiker's drinking water at one go. The hiker gets sick because he's just drank a month's worth of pathogens all at once.

Unless the water stinks or is visibly putrid, I don't treat the water at all. I try to be careful about how I collect it, but other than that trust my body to handle the small doses of contaminants as they come. I also use a common sense approach to toiletries and keeping my hands clean. This seems to work well.

I've run into a lot of hikers that at some point in their hiking careers have had intestinal distress and most of them attribute the cause to drinking untreated water. Backcountry equipment retailers assiduously educate hikers about water safety and are able to sell millions of dollars worth of water treatment gadgets or chemicals every year. It's a lucrative part of their business. They sell filters, pumps, straws, tablets, chemicals, Ultra-Violet emitting cups and pens. But it's difficult to know how much more effective all this paraphernalia is compared to the simple application of common sense.

Common sense may be equally effective in preventing diarrhea for hikers, but it's not all that profitable for the backcountry gear industry.

Back into the mountains, it was getting cold and windy again. We stopped to camp for the night at a spot called Camp 549 (549 miles up the trail from Mexico). There was a makeshift wooden bench, several old lawn chairs, a water cache, and a couple empty plastic buckets labeled 'Hiker Food'. It also had a great view out over the valley and Edwards Air Force Base.

We had been there for an hour or so, had our tents up and dinner eaten when a black pickup truck came grinding up the dirt road just beyond the camp. "We'll be right back!" the driver yelled to us. The truck went up the road, found a turnaround and came back. Don was a 60-ish guy with long blonde hair under a drover's hat, a smiling weathered face, and noticeable hand tremors. If a surfer boy went to the mountains and stayed there until he grew old, he'd look like Don. Which is pretty much what happened.

Don and his wife Emily had come up the mountain to check on the 'camp', see if there were any hikers that needed to get into town or the hospital, and to restock the 'Hiker Food' boxes. Kool-Aid, cookies, bananas, hard-boiled eggs, 20 gallons of fresh water. Emily said they liked to help, Don agreed and also pointed out that he didn't like having people dying of thirst on his property.

"A lot of people are afraid to walk in the snow up north in the Sierras," he said, "so they start the hike late and by the time they get here, it's hot and all the springs are dry. I've taken several to the hospital."

I asked how they came to live here in the mountains.

"My family lived in Los Angeles when I was a kid in 1975 and we didn't have much money. One day, my dad saw a two-line ad in the classified section of the paper about land for sale up here in the Tehachapi. So we came up here that weekend to have a look, and one of the pieces of property had this spring on it and the water was good.

"My folks had some money saved up, enough to put some money down but things were tight and they wouldn't be able to make the monthly payments. So my dad got all us kids together, me and my two brothers and sister, and said. ' Look, I think this land could really be something for the family. It's good land, in good country. Pinyon pines, mountain meadows, spring water and wild horses- a different way to live than here in the city. I've done the down payment, but I'm tapped out. You kids all have jobs after school now, and if each of you can contribute $25 a month each for the mortgage payments, the land will be yours'.

"So that's what we did. I took Emily here on our first date and showed her the land."

"He said, 'I'm going to live here in the mountains someday', " said Emily. "And I said, 'Where will you build your house?' Don pointed to a ridge and said, 'Right over there' So I told him, 'Then I'll live there with you.' That was 42 years ago. Sometimes, you just know, you know?"

The next day we walked past their house on the ridge by the spring with Pinyon pines overlooking wild horses in a meadow below. You can tell by looking that it's been a pretty good place to live. Sometimes you just know, you know?

LIZARD TAILS AND SNAFFLEHOUNDS

Miles on Trail... 530

Cool Breeze and I had settled into a daily routine in the desert that had been netting us between twenty to twenty-five miles per day. We'd wake up each morning at about 5:30, heat water for coffee and cereal, and pack camp. 6:30 would see us on the trail. Cool breeze is faster than me in the mornings so he would go out front and I would lollygag around behind. Somewhere around noon I'd overtake him, we'd discuss a target campsite for the evening, and then I'd stay out front for most of the remainder of the day. We would shoot for being into camp by 5pm.

To keep morale up, especially in the desert sections that to me were unfamiliar and unwelcoming, we decided that whining, griping, and complaining would be constrained daily to the 3 o'clock hour. Early on Cool Breeze developed an irritating afternoon habit of falling off the pace. I'm not sure he ever really came to comprehend the seriousness or sanctity of griping hour and how important it was that we spend that quality time together on the trail.

It's hot, dusty, grimy, salty, sweaty; and my watch reads 3 o'clock. Where's Cool Breeze? I scan the switchbacks behind and see him ambling along about a mile back. Even at this distance, I can see that he's totally unconcerned.

I watch him for a while and make a mental calculation. If I just wait for him here most of griping hour will be over before he's close enough to hear anything. I turn around and head back down the trail in the direction I had just come from.

"This trail is really ticking me off!" I say when the gap is closed to within earshot. "It's totally inefficient."

"So you decided to retrace a bunch of it to tell me how inefficient it is?" he asked, obviously failing to understand the situation.

"Dang right!" I answered. There was a brief struggle as I maneuvered to get behind him on the trail. I'd learned from experience that if I'm in front of Cool Breeze during griping hour, he'll just stop walking.

Come to think of it, I have to deploy the get-behind maneuver with my own son Matthew. I once used an entire griping hour to detail the many shortcomings of crunchy style peanut butter. Matthew spent the hour stabbing pine cones with his hiking stick and chucking them over his shoulder at me. I'm not sure he understands the importance or sanctity of griping hour either.

"You know what I've been doing all day?" I asked Cool Breeze's back. "Looking at my watch. You know why? I'll tell you.

"If you wear an analog watch like I do with hands on it you can tell what direction you're facing. Did you know that? Well, you hold your watch in front of you and bring it up to your sternum so 6 o'clock is touching your chest and 12 is away. Then you look at your shadow and rotate your body around until the hour hand, you know the short one, is pointing at your shadow's head. When you do that, you're facing north.

"And you know what direction the trail has been going all day? Not North. It's been going east, west, south, anything but north. We're supposed to be going north you know."

No response.

"Did you know I googled walking directions from Campo to Neenach when we were in cell range? And you know what it said? It said it should take us 9 days. Do you know how long we've been on this trail to do that? Three weeks! It's true!"

He mumbled something and started fumbling around in his pockets. I'm not stupid, he was looking for his earplugs again. I put a little less distance between me and his backpack. "You know I do mapping analysis for work and there is a tool called least cost path analysis. What you do is create a set of logical parameters for the computer to apply to a terrain model to find the most efficient path between two points. I've been looking at how this trail lays over the terrain here and I'm convinced that there is no set of parameters, slope, distance, aspect, maintainability, or aesthetics that can create a trail layout like the one we've been following all day. None! You'd have to introduce some randomizing factor to do anything this dumb! I swear, when I get home I'm going to do it to check!"

"So you want a tattoo on your neck? " he asked. "I had a girlfriend once that had tattoo on her neck. "

Was he ever listening? Oh yeah, earplugs.

"It was some pinkish heart thing with flowers and greenish bunnies around it. Right on the back of her neck. I said to her, 'are you nuts? You could have gotten meningitis or paralyzed getting a tattoo on the back of your neck like that!'

"But she didn't care, she was proud of it. Anytime you were having a conversation and she couldn't think of something to say, she would turn around backwards so you would have to look at her neck tattoo. She wore twin braids in her hair so you could see it better, and always wore blouses with deep neck lines on the back. Thought it was demure or something. But it was like talking to Pippi Longstocking with her head on backwards. Drove me crazy."

The woman apparently had many other character flaws, because he kept on complaining. But I didn't hear him. I had stopped walking.

Jeff, my Airbnb host in Wrightwood, had a 1970's trail guidebook for the San Gabriel mountains. In it were black and white photos of gently winding paths through stately and serene forests. Most of these forests no longer exist. Instead there are hundreds of square miles of cactus, sagebrush, and scrub oak growing in mineralized soil under the charred skeletons of pines and cedar. The deserts have crept up the slopes of the mountains and in most cases have conquered them completely.

The forests of the seventies exist today only in rare and sparsely scattered copses and small valleys. Walking out of the desert and into a patch of these untouched trees is like being delivered from purgatory. Under the trees it's green, shaded, and cool. There are squirrels chewing nuts out of pine cones and birdsong amongst the branches. For a short time you realize how wonderful these mountains must have been forty years ago.

Today most of the hike through Southern California is hot, dusty, and dirty. As you walk sand, grit, and ash works its way through your clothes and socks. It sticks to anything sweaty and turns to grime. It gets into your shoes, your ears, your nose, your eyes.

I had taken gray translucent water bottles for the trip. At home these work great. You can fill them with snow and the translucent plastic creates a greenhouse effect that melts the snow into ice water. But here in the desert they heat the water to about the same temperature as if it had just come out of a horse. It's an unsatisfying method to quench a thirst.

Daryl, the fireman that I had met in Green Valley, told me that basically forests in Southern California come in two types- those that have burned or those that are about to burn. These about-to-burn forests are either drought weakened and beetle killed pines or manzanita scrub. When ignited the pines burn like gasoline; the manzanita like rocket fuel. There's really no way to put one of these fires out, so the best they can hope for is to contain them. They choose a ridge several miles down wind and hack out a fire line and set back fires. Sometimes the fire break works and sometimes the fire jumps the ridge and keeps running. Either way a lot of forest is burned quickly.

And here's the thing- it's not coming back. The fires burn so hot that all the organics in the soil are immolated. The soil is cooked sterile and becomes hydrophobic, unable to absorb or hold any moisture. Before the fire even the mature trees in the forests were drought stressed to the edge of survival. And afterwards no forest regeneration is possible. Even if there were seeds that managed to survive the fire and germinate in the mineralized soil, without the shade created by their parents there's no way for seedlings to survive. So the desert takes over. The squirrels and songbirds are replaced by snakes and lizards.

I had developed a particular distaste for lizards. Dozens of times each mile, I would come across a lizard sunning itself on the trail. As I approached, the lizard would skitter away to cover under some rock or other. I noticed early on that the skittering lizards would always have their necks cocked, looking back over a shoulder as they ran to watch my feet. Their eyes work independently; one eye on the threat and the other on the escape route. By way of experimentation, I found that if you bring your hiking stick over the top so that it suddenly appears in front of the lizard's forward-looking eye that you can momentarily freeze the lizard in place. He will remain frozen for about three tenths of a second while his lizard brain runs the algorithm to decide which threat to ignore and which direction the new escape route will be. A person can use this three-tenth second pause to step on the lizard's tail. When the algorithm is run and the new course computed, the lizard takes off again- only this time leaving most of his tail behind under your foot. Over the last 500 miles, I had left dozens of short-tailed lizards in my wake. It's not something I'm proud of, but neither am I repentant.

Back home there's a little critter that mountaineers call a snafflehound. Most people know them as kangaroo or common pack rats. Climbers are often forced to bivy in tight spots amongst the rocks and crevices below a mountain's summit and at night, snafflehounds sneak out to chew through, pillage, and steal climbers' food and equipment. They will take anything they can get their little paws on, food, toilet paper, car keys, headlamp batteries, socks, shoelaces, -anything. They'll take these back through the rocks to their nests, large middens of collected twigs, grasses, and snafflehound treasures of all kinds. Climbers are often forced to stay awake all night to guard their stuff. Snafflehounds are relentless and tenacious nuisances for tired climbers trying to get some rest in already uncomfortable conditions. I had always considered them to be stinky little pests before.

But somehow snafflehounds survived the southern forest fires and over the miles of deserts my feelings towards them evolved. As they are about the only other mammals in the desert, I came to think of them as sort of kindred cousins.

Over the last 500 miles of walking it was not uncommon to see a dead and bloating snafflehound alongside the trail that had been killed by a rattlesnake. Twin puncture wounds over the snafflehound's kidneys would ooze a black fluid where the venom went in. The sight disturbed and angered me more each time I saw it.

"How dare you!" I'd want to say to the rattlesnake, "How dare you! You can do nothing worthwhile, so you kill my little cousin to steal his nest. You are jealous of his industry and resourcefulness, so you kill his family and take his home. Your kind had 200 million year's dominion over this earth and you did nothing. It's our turn now, and we've painted caves, created music, written books, and invented toasters. You shouldn't even be here, the desert shouldn't be here, and these mountains should be blanketed by forest.

"This climate change thing will be no more than a hiccup in our history. The groundwork is already lain and over the next generations, we mammals will take care of this global warming thing, the forests will come back to these mountains, and you and your stupid stubby-tailed lizard friends will be forced back down to your old scabland habitats. Only then you'll find that they're covered with our solar panels. Maybe we'll carve out some reservations for you to live on, or maybe we won't.

"You will kill no more mammals, Snake."

That's my hopeful view of the future anyway, that we'll get our act together and prioritize survival over profits.

Kennedy Meadows marks the end of the southern California deserts and the beginning of the High Sierra. It's also a dividing point of sorts for PCT hikers. From Kennedy Meadows northwards, there's more water, but more difficult mountainous and remote trail. Hikers need to be more self-reliant; towns are farther apart and you meet fewer fellow hikers on the trail.

Cool Breeze had apprehensions of the trail going north and proposed several times that we stay put in Kennedy Meadows for a week or two, wait for some hikers that we knew were coming in from behind us, and then put a team together to take on the Sierras. I couldn't see the point in it- why did we need a team, when everyone was self-sufficient and carrying their own gear? Yes, there would be snow and ice-covered passes up to 13,000 feet in elevation- but nobody would carry rope, pickets, or climbing gear that far in anyway.

"What would a 'team' do?" I asked. "Why waste time putting a team together? Especially if we need to wait around for slower fellows that we passed weeks ago? What will waiting accomplish?" Cool Breeze's proposal didn't make sense to me.

Later on though, it did.

Kennedy Meadows has no cell service, no motels, and no trail angels to take in PCT hikers. There're not many people that live there, and most that do are "Trumpers". Trumpers find identity by kindling and cherishing their belief of victimhood at the hands of some ethnic group or other. There's a dearth of blacks, Muslims, or Mexicans in Kennedy Meadows so the PCT hikers had to stand in as targets for their contempt and hatred.

There were a number of signs posted, 'No Trespassing', 'Gun Control Means Using Both Hands', 'Make America Great Again!', 'Don't Even Think About Camping Here'. Weird. "Who would even think of camping there, Dingdong?" I thought. "Your little patch of dirt and tumbleweeds in the middle of this nowhere has rusted car bodies and broken beer bottles all over it. Get real."

We were allowed to camp in a dirt parking lot beside a tavern owned by some rare-for-Kennedy-Meadows-PCT-friendly folks. The tavern had spotty wi-fi, so I spent a lot of time hiding in the woods typing for the blog on my phone offline. When I came out of the woods to the tavern, Cool Breeze caught me and took me aside.

"The kids hiking with Chameleon are leaving the trail for at least a couple weeks. I know you don't want to wait for guys for a stronger team, but I really think we should ask her if she'd join up with us for the next section."

"Sure," I said. We had met Chameleon a couple weeks ago. She camped with us one night after she had out-hiked her companions and we had seen her on the trail off and on ever since. She got her trail name in 2015 hiking the Appalachian Trail for her cheerful adaptability. She wasn't super fast, but was steady and experienced. But what really made her special was, that as far as I could tell, she was the only person younger than thirty that Cool Breeze actually liked.

Chameleon looks slow but isn't. Half of her hair is brown, the rest cheerfully colored with Raspberry Kool-Aid. She wears a black narrow backpack so from behind you can see her torso and arms sticking out from the sides (rare for PCT hikers), making her look wider than average. She wears a fanny pack spun around to the front that hangs over her waist belt buckle, purplish spandex pants cut to mid calf length, and blue ankle gaiters over wide trail shoes. She walks with a short, quick, slightly toed-out gait. Her demeanor may be Chameleon-like, but the first impression I got was 'Penguin'. A happy penguin.

Chameleon was agreeable and would be ready to go after she picked up her mailed box and ice axe the next day. I bought a set of crampons (spikes for walking on ice) that fit to my tennis shoes that I found at the general store and went back to the tavern to kill some time. Karate Kid was out at a picnic table also killing time, in a novel and interesting way. He'd taken the dirty shoe and sock off of one foot, and was holding his toes back with one hand. His cell phone was in selfie mode and propped on the picnic table bench in front of him so he had a good view of the filthy sole of his foot. He had his sewing kit out and was trying to stitch the ragged edges of his ruptured blisters back together. I got a couple more beers for us and came back to supply Karate Kid my hearty support and expert advice.

One more day of forced immobility, and we'd be off and into the Sierras.

POST HOLES AND ICE WATER

Miles on Trail... 624

It was great getting out of Kennedy Meadows, the first couple miles were desert-ish, but it was clearly apparent that we were moving up into a new biome. I still saw lizards that first day out, but not many. The last lizard I saw on the PCT north of Kennedy Meadows had a short tail before I even got to him. Swear to God it's true.

The second day in, I developed mild case of altitude sickness, with a headache and nausea, messing up our plan a bit. At a lunch break I told them that I wanted to camp three miles short of the day's goal so I could sleep one more time below 9,000 feet elevation.

"No one is left behind in the Sierras," Cool Breeze said. "We'll all stop."

Chameleon worked out the math and mentioned that to get over Forrester Pass before noon, forty-six miles ahead, meant that we'd have to go even farther in the next couple of days. It would be longer and more difficult if we stopped short now. Also, the elevations would be greater, the air thinner, and the snow more problematic; all of which would make it more difficult to get back on track.

"If we don't make our miles, we'll have to post-hole all the way up Forrester," Chameleon said.

"So. Then we'll post-hole", Cool Breeze said.

I felt too miserable to participate in the discussion, so I left them behind and went on down the trail to the lower campsite as fast as I could. I found a shaded place to lie down, drank some water, took some pills, went to sleep.

"There you are! You should leave your backpack by the trail if you're going to quit walking." Cool Breeze was ticked off at me. "Walked all over hell looking for you", he said.

"I'm right here where I told him I'd be," I thought but didn't say anything. He seemed too angry, and I needed a little more time lying flat. About an hour later I felt good enough to move but when I looked over, I could see Cool Breeze's tent set up. Chameleon had laundry strung up and drying between a couple trees, and was working on some equipment maintenance. It looked like we weren't going any farther today.

So I put my new crampons on my tennis shoes and tried them out, scrabbling up a steep-sided boulder. Cool Breeze came over to watch, scowling.

"What are you doing?" he asked.

"Trying these things out. Never put crampons on tennis shoes before, so I wanted to see what they could do before I needed them. The shoes want to roll a little," I said.

"That's stupid. Nobody walks on snow that steep," he said. "They would all die!" He went back to his tent.

"Yeah they do. If it's not steep, why even put them on?" I thought. But kept quiet as he didn't seem to be in the mood for discussion. I felt bad that we were wasting daylight without making any miles because of me.

The next day I was determined not to hold us up so kept my foot on the gas. I ran into Chameleon's former Houdini and Turtle Hair, the ones leaving the trail, a little after lunch. They were stopped at a side trail out, enjoying the sun. I wanted to chat and wish them well in case we didn't see each other again. Chameleon came up and then Cool Breeze, not too long after.

"A guy just passed us on his way to the side trail out of here," Turtle Hair said. "He told us there's too much snow just a mile ahead. He's getting off the PCT here."

We said our goodbyes and went on up the trail to see what there was to see. Cool Breeze warned that we should stay close together when we got to the snow. I nodded and got on with it, still anxious to make sure I wasn't the weak link two days in a row.

There were a few snow patches on the trail, nothing really to worry about. Some you could get around, some you could walk over, and some you just had to post-hole through. For those unfamiliar with the term, post-holing is what you do when you try to go snowshoeing without snowshoes. You take a step onto crusty, firm looking snow that only momentarily supports your weight. It's fantastic exercise, because the snow stays solid just long enough for you to lift the combined weight of you and your backpack up with one leg- then collapses completely. Your foot is now at the bottom of an eighteen to thirty-six inch deep 'post-hole'. Then you lift your other foot out of its hole to the top of the snow's surface, single-leg press your weight up, the snow collapses, repeat. I stopped at the first real patch of this stuff.

"The trick to this stuff," I said when Chameleon and Cool Breeze got there, " is smooth weight transfer and ankle control. Try to shift your weight smoothly from one foot to the other so you don't shock the snow's crust. And try to control your ankle to keep your foot square on the surface as you shift your weight. If you do punch through, try to keep your foot completely level and maybe you won't punch through as far."

"And you're better off walking where nobody has tried walking before," Cool Breeze said, stepping up onto an untracked snow bank. He punched through and fell awkwardly, his backpack pulling him to the side. His knee bent at least thirty degrees sideways.

"Are you okay?" I asked. I hoped that plastic knees could withstand that sort of thing. It didn't look good.

"F- this!" he yelled. "What are you guys doing?"

"I was thinking of continuing on north," I said.

"I'm going back. Enough of this crap."

"Do you want us to go with you? Are you sure you're okay?"

"Just go without me. I'm not doing this stupid stuff!" he said. He turned around, headed south down the trail without another word. Chameleon and I looked after him and then at each other.

"Should we go after him?" I asked.

"I don't think he'd like that," she said.

"What do you want to do?"

"Go north," said Chameleon.

This episode bewildered me then and has bothered me ever since. I knew Cool Breeze's real name and the last town he lived in. But his stuff was in a storage container, he had no mailing address, refuses to use a computer, and doesn't have a cell phone. The last I saw him he was walking on the PCT heading south. Where he is now, I don't know. Will I ever see him again? I don't know that either.

For the next couple of days the snow didn't get worse, but it didn't really get any better either. It was manageable. It got colder, though. Again, I wore all my clothes including raingear and extra socks while I slept- or rather, while I tried to sleep. Campfires aren't allowed in the Sierras over 10,000 ft, and even if they were there wasn't anything to burn anyway. The landscape was pretty bleak. When the sun went down, so did the temperature.

The trail steadily climbs and passes over the foot of Mount Whitney's western flank. There was a twelve-mile side trail to Whitney's 14,500-foot summit, 3,500 feet higher up, and a few PCT hikers were milling about the trail intersection trying to decide whether they should try for the summit or not. It was cold and windy and didn't seem a very difficult decision to me. Up there, it would be even colder and windier.

Chameleon and I walked past without stopping. I don't know that we even talked about it. The trail crossed several icy streams that we had to wade through. Our laces froze in their grommets and our feet were cold in our tennis shoes. These stream crossings were especially irksome. Summers in the Sierras can be really hot and dry so the trail is routed to cross several streams; trickling, ankle-deep little moments of refreshment for the summer hiker. But now in the early spring they were mid-thigh deep with ice water.

When it's that cold, it's preferable to find another way to get past the stream. If there were no other ways around, we would look for a shallow place to cross. Wide and shallow is much better than narrow and deep. Surveying crossings, we'd use the rule of four- at the fastest part of the crossing, estimate its speed in feet per second. Then multiply that by its depth in feet. If the product is more than four, look for another place to cross. Sometimes we would have to walk the stream banks pretty far, and in that bleak landscape- snow covered and cold, time was precious.

Six miles south of Forrester Pass we couldn't find any safe place to cross a stream, and even though it was only mid-afternoon we had to camp there for the night. No one likes crossing a stream in the morning right after getting out of a warm sleeping bag, but close to their source streams sort of breathe- they swell in the afternoons when sun is up melting snow and shrink at nights when the temperature plummets. So the next morning the stream was shallow and relatively easy to cross.

Even so, you can't just plow ahead and wade through- shoes and socks would freeze as you continue walking in the snow, and your pants would freeze to your legs in the wind. You need to cross without your pants or socks. So we took them off, stuffed them in our backpacks, slipped our tennis shoes back on over our bare feet and stepped into the ice water. Skin exposed to the wind stung; everything underwater was excruciating. It was temping to try stepping up onto the rocks sticking up above the surface, but we didn't dare- they were verglassed, covered in ice. It's best to keep waddling your way across to the other side. Once there, we took off our backpacks to sit on them and dried ourselves with camp towels before putting our pants and shoes back on. I had gallon-size Ziploc bags for these events. To keep our socks dry, we'd pull the plastic bags over our socks before putting our shoes back on. That last crossing was an especially cold one; to keep from chattering I had clenched my teeth so hard that my jaw muscles hurt.

Finding a safe stream crossing had put us a couple miles off the trail, which was pretty much useless at this point since we couldn't see it under the snow anyway.

North of us, the valley ended in a wide cirque, an intimidating semi-circle of granite walls topped with jagged peaks. Forrester Pass went over that wall between two of those peaks, but for the life of me I couldn't see where. All the gaps looked impossible. I used a mapping phone app that gives you precise bearings in degrees, and got out my compass to sight the pass. The compass pointed to one of the cirque's narrower tooth gaps, just east of center.

"How does it look to you?" Chameleon asked, hoping that my mountaineering experience could offer some encouragement.

"The compass says that right there is Forrester Pass," I said, pointing, "and that looks like death. Hmm." I turned around and pointed. "And going back the way we came looks like starvation." To get here we had had four days of post-holing and stream crossings and our backpacks had food enough left in them for another day and a half. We were already rationing and ravenous- the cold made us constantly hungry.

Chameleon frowned, looked north. "When you say 'death', do you mean 'certain' death or just 'death' death?" she asked.

I sighted the invisible pass again. "Uh, death death?"

"Well okay then," she said. "If it's just 'death' death, let's go over the pass. Running out of food really stinks, you know."

Back in the day, I had taught a mountaineering course at a community college for six years, and I had always told the students that it's perfectly okay to back off if the terrain forces you to. What's not okay is to let your fears of the unknown ahead to turn you around before you even get there. Safe and successful mountaineering, and backcountry travel in general, is largely fear management. You know, knowing when you should be scared; and at the moment right there where we stood there was nothing to fear. Ahead was only the unknown, and it was best to continue on a bit to have a closer look.

Closer, Forrester Pass looked a little more encouraging. There was a thin ribbon of snow that reached to the top of the gap between two granite peaks. With crampons and an ice axe, any snow that stays put and accumulates on a mountainside should be passable. But it was definitely steep, icy, and little intimidating; what mountaineers call sporty. I put on my crampons and borrowed Chameleon's ice axe and went up the ribbon, kicking little foot holds in the snow as I went. It was about as steep as a ladder and had the consistency of stiff Styrofoam, pretty much perfect conditions. At the top of the chute was the pass proper and a view to the north that was more welcoming; easier slopes getting down the other side. I left my backpack at the pass and went back down the ribbon the way up I had come to get Chameleon.

I put on Chameleon's backpack and gave her back the ice axe, and then we started up, Chameleon in the lead. I stayed close, really close. Each time she pulled her foot out of foot hold, I'd replace it with one of my own. It was like tailgating on a ladder.

"Don't climb so fast," I said.

"Quit pushing me, then." Chameleon said. "I don't like your panting on my backside."

"I need to stay close," I said. "In case you slip and fall I don't want any space between us. If you build up speed before you hit me, I won't be able to stop us. We'd scream down the chute and hit the rocks down there."

"I could scream right now."

"We're doing good. Just look at the exact spots you're putting your hands, your feet, your ice axe. Stay in balance, create a rhythm, breathe. I'm right behind you."

At 13,200 feet above sea level, Forrester pass is the highest point on the Pacific crest trail. It looked and felt every bit of that. From the top and looking over the other side, it was a relief to see that the terrain was more forgiving. I took off my crampons while Chameleon took some selfies to post. I thought about the lowest point on the Pacific crest trail some 1,800 miles north of us at the Columbia River. I hoped that things would work out that I could walk there.

As we descended, the sun climbed and the snow lost its nice Styrofoam consistency. It became rough work. The nice Styrofoam surface quit supporting us and we started post-holing again. As the day got warmer, the post-holing got worse and even less fun than usual. By late afternoon, the snow deteriorated to the point that even post-holing became impossible. It was more like wading through mashed potatoes. But we had gotten over the pass and were headed downhill.

That night we found a campsite where we could have a fire. It was luxurious to get warm and to finally get our clothes dried. We hadn't seen anyone but each other for the last couple days and we were spent, physically and emotionally. The day had made the wilderness seem especially vast and had us feeling especially small and vulnerable. We set our tents up almost touching that night. Chameleon uses an inflatable air mattress that's irritatingly loud; whenever she moves it sounds as if she's crunching up corn flakes inside a squeaky inner tube. But that night it was oddly comforting to hear her rustling about.

The next morning Chameleon told me that I had snored like a chainsaw all night, and that she'd never slept better. We ate our last candy bars and hiked out a side trail seven miles east to Independence to resupply and regroup.

51

OSPREY AND SKIPPING AHEAD

Miles on Trail... 632

I t started snowing again in the Sierras after we got out.

It turned out that the Pacific's atmospheric river had shifted south, so instead of sending rain to Seattle like it usually does, it was sending snow to the Sierras. Sort of a May miracle for Californians. But not so good for hikers trying to hike through. What to do?

Some hikers are 'purists' and their personal convictions dictate that they stick to the trail, south to north, no matter what. Mushroom, who I met at back in Big Bear was one of these, and we met him at the Independence trailhead going back in as we were coming out. Later, we heard how he and his party were doing – they made six miles a day.

So again, what to do? Well, first off, Chameleon and I decided to stick together. We got along well, and hiked about the same speed. I'm not an expert in long distance hiking, resupply logistics, or trail condition research through social media. Chameleon is. She's not a fan of traversing steep snow, or backcountry navigation when there's no trail to be seen. I am. The trail went more smoothly when we deferred to each other's strengths, and decided to keep it up.

We decided to skip ahead 320 miles by bus and to hike the Sierras north to south. Chameleon had reports that the snow was more manageable at the northern end of the Sierra and if we started from there, it would give the snowpack a couple more weeks to melt down and consolidate before we got back in to the heart of the mountains again. A night in town, and we'd be off.

I had paid twenty-five dollars to sleep on a twin sized mattress at the top of a bunkbed, one of four crammed into the room. All the bunks were full. We shared a single bathroom. There was a German guy in the bunk below me; Chameleon in a lower bunk at the other end of the room. Opposite Chameleon, also in a lower bunk, was the only other woman in the group. She had come to California from Latvia to climb California's big wall granite. While there, she met a fellow eastern European, a guy from Estonia, also on a budget-conscious big wall vacation. Their native tongues were different, but were able to communicate with each other in English and it seemed to be working out alright. They were splitting the twenty-five dollar a night rent, sharing a bunk.

They had returned to the room from a shopping trip as I was getting clothes from my pack to take to a laundromat. Their shopping bag held the contents of the next day's breakfast, lunch, and dinner- eight Pork 'n Beans cans that they had gotten on sale two for a dollar. It was their sixth consecutive day benefiting from the price markdown. They were healthy and cheerful to chat with, but just sitting in the same room with them made my eyes water. They were gas assassins, silent and deadly.

That night I opened a window and tried sleeping with my nose touching the screen. It didn't work. Outside streetlights lit the room dimly and I could see the cheerful assassins blissfully spooning on their mattress together. Everyone else had their blankets pulled up over their heads. I tried that. It didn't work. I had to get outside. My watch read two a.m.

The hostel had converted a detached garage into an outdoor lounge area of sorts. There were a couple threadbare old sofas, the kind that you would find sitting alongside the road, board games with pieces missing and empty beer bottles on coffee tables in there. Old bicycles and plastic kayaks were stuffed in the open attic above the rafters. Prayer flags and Christmas lights hung below them. On the walls were hung old bed sheets and an old broken electric clock with its hands permanently positioned at 4:20.

I had thought to get more sleep by lying on one of the sofas outside in the garage, but there was an old man sitting on one of the sofas. He was cradling a light blue ukulele with a little ivory shark on the fretboard. He had bleary gray and bloodshot eyes under prodigious white eyebrows. What I could see of his face was sun crinkled, but mostly what I noticed was long white hair and an even longer white beard. He wore a floppy desert hat and hiker clothes, the kind of clothes that look like they usually go a long ways between washings. His name was Osprey.

"You couldn't sleep either?" he asked. On the coffee table in front of him was half a bottle of whiskey and a six-pack. Four bottles were already empty and he was working on the fifth.

"Well, I guess I'm not sleeping tonight either," I said. I sat down on a sofa facing him.

"I thought those German guys in the hostel making all their plans were funny," he said. "That's not how it works. You can't plan everything like that. Planning never works."

He took another pull from the whiskey bottle, put it down. Picked up a beer and chased it. He played three cords on his ukulele, but if it was a tune I needed more notes than that to identify it.

"Can you believe a cop hassled me in town today?" he asked. "Thought I was homeless. Do I look homeless to you? Well I'm not. I'm a hiker. That's what I do. This is my seventh time hiking the PCT."

"Well where is home?" I asked. "When you're not on the trail I mean?"

"It doesn't really matter," he said. "But my mail and stuff goes to my ex-wife's and her husband's house. They keep it for me until I come back around. I have friends all over, so I am NOT homeless. There's always some place I can go." He strummed a few more pointless notes. If it was a song, I couldn't identify that one either.

"These last late storms in the Sierra though," he said shaking his head. "Stayed at my brother's place in Bakersfield. Shared a room there with my niece, until it became a hassle. Huh." He strummed a couple more notes, thinking about it. "She's Twenty-three. Ought to have her own place by now anyway."

He frowned to himself, perhaps hearing the irony of what he had just said. He took another pull from the whiskey bottle, put it down, chased it with the last of beer number five.

"I know in my head that someday soon I'll have to stop walking, but my heart doesn't know it. It won't know it till it actually happens, and when that happens I just don't know what will happen. What I'll do, you know. It's pretty much all I've ever done, the only thing I've done that makes me feel alive when I'm doing it."

Another couple of pointless notes on the ukulele. I wished he'd actually play something coherent, but realized he never would.

"But I can feel that it's gonna happen and it's gonna happen soon and I just don't know what's going to happen when it happens," he said.

I thought of Cool Breeze, and the vision of his last northbound step on the PCT replayed in my mind. I had an idea that Cool Breeze felt his happening was going to happen before it happened, and that's why he was so skittery and anxious in the weeks leading up to it. I hoped I would see him again to find out what he was up to now.

Osprey plonked a few more pointless notes. Noise without meaning. It was irritating. I've never been able to really kick the dairy farmer habit and my sleep window closes at 4 a.m., and time was getting short. I had been chased out of bed by the farting couple and now was being kept awake by a maudlin old man drinking boilermakers by himself and uselessly strumming a ukulele. Why didn't he have something else to do?

I had spent my whole life dreaming of hiking the PCT and hoping if I worked hard enough that someday I would be able to go. There is always something that needs to be done and people that are counting on you to do it. What kind of life do you need live to be able to hike the PCT seven times I wondered? Probably the kind of life where you get your mail at your ex-wife's house and share a room with your niece until you are kicked out.

'Judge not, that you be not judged. For with the judgment you pronounce you will be judged,' I know. But I judged that he had probably lived his life the same way he played the ukulele. Poorly and pointlessly. With a nod, I got up and walked out into the street, wandered around till daylight. And at 6:30 Chameleon and I took the bus out of town to Tahoe.

Some months later I ran into Chameleon's hiking friends Houdini and Turtle Hair in Yosemite. While Chameleon and I had skipped ahead to get around the late snowfalls, they had gone home to wait out the melt to get back on the trail. We had a chat and shared news. One of the things that Houdini told me was that old Osprey had died in the Hostel California the day after our late night conversation.

Funny how that worked out, I thought. Something that night had made him uneasy, and reflective. At the time I had attributed his maudlin meanderings to the boilermakers that he was drinking. But it may very well have been the incipient heart attack that had created his mood. When he was fretting about "what would happen when it happened," he thought the 'what would happen' was that he'd have to stop hiking the trail. Well, he was right about that.

Like he said, planning never works. You never really know what will happen when it happens.

I have a friend at home named Kenny. Forty years ago he was helping his friend put a new foundation under his house when a jack skewed sideways and he was crushed under a house beam. He was paralyzed, his legs useless since the accident. He's been in a wheelchair with a colostomy and cath bags ever since.

He told me that if he was able, he would be hiking the PCT with me himself. But the way things happened, he can't. Kenny didn't make plans for what would happen after he became paralyzed; you can't plan for things like that. But he did make plans for what would happen if his life ever became useless.

Kenny has a pistol ready to use whenever he judges that his life has become useless. He's had that gun ready at hand for forty years, but here's the thing- he's always been too busy to use it. He's rebuilt engines, raised children, listened to problems and given sought-after advice. He knows everyone in town, their children, and their children's children. He's buried two wives and most of his friends. I've never heard him fretting or whining about what to do, because he's always too busy doing something that needs to be done.

Kenny is 84 years old, and when he dies, he'll be leaving a long list of unfinished work to be done. Kenny's to-do list will probably keep a lot of us busy for months after his funeral. Kenny will be a hell of a lot more trouble than Osprey was.

You can never know everything there is to know about a person. But you can think about what you do know and wonder about the rest. And one of the things I wonder about sometimes is whose life I would rather live, Osprey's or Kenny's. The one walked and walked, but was cherished by no one. The other doesn't, but is valued by everyone. It's a tough question.

But I do know one thing. It's doubtful that I'll be able to outlive my to-do list. At the rate I'm getting through it, and the way it keeps getting longer, it looks like I'll be a lot of trouble when I die. You can plan on that at least.

SLOGGING DAMP

Miles on Trail... 679

There was another hostel in Tahoe, but after the experience at the Hostel California, I wasn't about to go there. I told Chameleon that she was welcome to stay that night in a two bed hotel room with me. I thought we should have 'the talk' so I started, but Chameleon cut me off. She was amused.

"As if," Chameleon said.

"As if, what?" I said, vaguely hurt.

"As if you're even close to my type."

"How's that?"

Chameleon rolled her eyes. "Well, for one thing you're older than my dad."

"Yeah, so?"

"And you're white."

The next morning we took an Uber to the trailhead at Echo Lake. Our plan to hike southbound through the Sierras from here wasn't going well. The snow started bad and got worse.

The snowpack in the Sierras was dismal- something like 20% of normal. So you'd think it would be easy to walk through it, but it's not so. Some of the Sierras routinely get 15 feet of snow or more per year; even if those areas only got 20% of normal, that's still about 4 feet of the stuff. We slogged through a lot of this waist deep mashed-potato snow north of Forrester Pass and it was more of the same here. The snow's lack of structure surprised me. I'm used to walking on snow, but Cascades snow. Cascades cement, it's often called. Spring in the North Cascades will have you walking on lots of deep snow; but snow that had been much deeper. The weight of the snow in a deep snowpack will compress the lower portion of the pack.

Then, as the snow melts off the top of the pack, water percolates down through the snow underneath. This compression and percolating water gives the spring snow in the Cascades a density that makes it relatively easy to walk through. Rarely at home do my feet sink over my boot tops.

But the waist deep snow that we walked through in the Sierras had no structure. It hadn't been compressed by a heavier snowpack. And it hadn't been melting or percolating meltwater through it either. If you had to traverse snow that was waist deep, that's pretty much how you had to do it- waist deep.

It's difficult to make your miles in this stuff. And if you don't make your miles, you run out of food before you get to your next resupply stop. Or, you have to carry more food on your back. The extra weight slows you down and makes your post-holing even more tiresome and time consuming.

"We're going to run out of food before we get to Sonora Pass at this rate," Chameleon said. We had only gone four miles and I wasn't ready to give up yet. I ignored her, sighted a new landmark, and post-holed to it. She was right, but I didn't have another plan.

"What should we do then?" I asked.

"Not this. Turn back. Regroup."

Going backwards just gravels me, but she was right. Slogging through deep snow and running out of food in the mountains three days short of a resupply would probably gravel me too.

We retraced our tracks most of the way, then a shortcut cross country to a highway where we could hitch a ride.

"Stand there, take off your pack, collapse your hiking sticks, look at the cars so people can see your face," Chameleon said. "They need to decide if they want to let you into their car. And really, would it hurt you to smile? You're killing me here. You look like a sad axe murderer that just lost his puppy or something."

Hitching is Chameleon's super power. She stands smiling next to her backpack, watching cars coming up the road. As the distance closes so that she can see through the glass she assesses the drivers. When she sees one she likes, she punches her fist out towards the car and pops her thumb up. This somehow causes the vehicle's brakes to lock up, tires squeal, and drivers' heads hit windshields. It's fast; she usually has a car pulled over before my under-developed smiling muscles cramp up.

She got us a ride back to town, and got to work at a McDonald's with free Wi-Fi. I just ate a hamburger.

"Ok. There's a party that just made it from Donner Pass to Sierra City and they said it was doable."

58

"Let's do that then," I said. "That's another eighty-five miles north," she said, "and people are getting off work now. We need to get back out there if we want a ride."

She got us a ride up the west shore of Lake Tahoe to a bus station. From there the bus took us to Squaw Valley, and then another hitch to Truckee. It was late, so the next morning Chameleon found a trail angel on the Facebook page to get us a ride to the ski area at Donner Pass.

The snow was better there, never more than knee deep. We made sixteen miles before a thunderstorm's sleet and hail forced us back into our tents. Intermittent thunderstorms, rain, sleet, and hail would be the norm for the next week and a half.

Monica and Matthew were making real sacrifices back home to allow me to make this trip. In addition, several of my friends and coworkers also worked hard so I could have a chance to make this hike. I truly appreciate all that they have done for me, and feel deeply the debt to them that I have accrued. So I'm hesitant to elaborate on what those two weeks of hiking was like. I have no right to gripe.

But please feel free to imagine for yourself what it was like to wear tennis shoes through knee deep snow, wading through streams of ice water, in the fog, or rain, or sleet. Or after sixteen or eighteen miles of it, what it's like to set up a soggy tent and to climb into a damp sleeping bag. Or how restful it is to mop up the water pooling inside your tent every hour or so throughout the night with your spare pair of socks and ringing them out the rain fly. This was life on the trail.

When we were hiking Chameleon's feet went numb, so sometimes she would look down and notice that one of her shoes had gone missing. When this happened she would have to turn back and walk the other way to find which post hole her shoe was at the bottom of. We lost a little time with these endeavors.

We made it to our next resupply town, Sierra City, only to find that the General Store was closed. So we got a ride to a gas station ten miles down the road and resupplied our packs with a week's worth of gas station fare. I filled my pack with cheese sticks and Pringles cans. Chameleon scored with a can of ready-to-spread chocolate cake frosting. It was weird to find cake frosting at a gas station, but she thought the ingredients- powdered sugar mixed with lard, could make for adequate hiking fuel. Then back to the trail.

CHAMELEON

Miles on Trail... 815

It snowed overnight, so there was really no way to keep our hands from freezing packing up camp. So they froze. We hiked the long downhill grade to Belden, and as they warmed their reanimation came with a painful bout of the screaming meemies.

We met trail runners on the switch backs coming up as we were going down. Meeting trail runners means you're someplace close to a road, relatively speaking anyway. Some of them do the darnedest things. I once met a trail runner on the PCT fifteen miles from the nearest trailhead at 8:00 in the morning. Think about that a minute. Even if he was making 5 miles an hour, he must have started running around 5:00 in the morning.

I know trail running is probably about one of the healthiest things you can do with yourself. It combines running (aerobics) over uneven terrain (balance) outside in a natural setting, which is also good for you. But the sport makes me a little nervous. Trail runners wear sporty shorts, stylish and flashy, and tiny backpacks or hip flasks that bob cheerfully along as they jog down the trail. Some wear their ponytails sticking jauntily out the back of a baseball cap. Call me paranoid, but the way they look and the way they move makes them big bouncy, kitty lures. And out in the wilderness, there are some big kitties.

A friend of mine is a mountain lion researcher and probably knows as much as there is to know about them. He calls them big, bad kitties. Their instincts are fine-tuned for stalking and ambush and he gave me a rule of thumb to understand their behavior- the '10-5-1 rule'. A big cat will typically sneak up behind ten targets for each attack launched, and it will take five attacks to make one successful kill. So even if you do attract a mountain lion's attention, chances are pretty good really, about fifty-to-one, that he won't kill you. Still, I think it's imprudent to dress yourself like a giant cat toy, plug in your ear buds, and then go bouncing along past one in the woods. My researcher friend has big googly eyes glued to the back of the hat he wears out on field forays. He knows those big, bad kitties, and says they behave better if they think they are being watched.

Anyway, I'd learned not to get too excited about seeing trail runners, it could still be a long ways to go yet. Children, perfume, water bottles carried in hand, and smokers, these were the sure tells that meant a trail's end is nearby. All we had so far were trail runners.

There's only about twenty people that live in Belden, so there is no grocery store for a resupply, which is disappointing when your backpack is filled with gas station junk food. But what it does have is the Belden Town Resort, an old mining outpost. The outbuildings have been converted to cabin rentals. The main building contains an antique shop, biker bar, and a restaurant. And the restaurant had burgers and fries. We went inside with our packs, took them off, and slid into a booth beside them.

"I'll have the Belden Burger, the large fries, salad with blue cheese dressing, and a Coke," I told the waiter guy.

"Pepsi okay?" he asked. Our waiter was a slight fair-haired guy, balding, with a single studded earring, and he looked at us as if he knew something we didn't.

"Sure, Pepsi is fine," I said.

"I'll have the same," said Chameleon.

"You got it," he said and sashayed off. He was bare-chested under a maroon velvet smoking jacket with no sleeves, and wore leopard print tights for pants. On his feet were shiny black patent shoes with silver buckles. He walked on tiptoe, and twisted his heels inward with each step, as if he were walking on a path of cigarette butts that needed to be snubbed. The motion was translated up to his rear, where there an odd large foxtail sticking out from his leopard-print pajama bottoms. It switched and swished festively as he walked.

"I feel like yanking that," I said to Chameleon.

Local historical trivia was printed on the paper placemats. Chameleon didn't look up. "I don't think you should do that," she said. "It's attached to a butt plug."

"A what?" I asked.

"A butt plug. It's attached to a butt plug," she said.

"How do you know that?" I asked.

"Because." Chameleon said. "From when I was in fourth grade through middle school my mother was a bookkeeper at an adult novelty shop. I used to go over there after school to visit. I've seen everything. They sold one there that had that exact tail on it."

I'm the parent of an elementary school student, and tried to imagine explaining that. I couldn't.

"So how did your Mom go about explaining butt plugs to you as a fourth grader?"
"I asked.

"How else? Frankly and honestly," Chameleon said. "She told me that some people just like the feeling of having something stuck up their butts. And those people could buy butt plugs. They would need some way to get them back out, so there's handles on them. And if you're going to have a handle on it sticking out, why not make it a pretty like a bushy fox tail?"

When the pretty bushy fox tail came back with our order Chameleon fell to it, but I hesitated. I was hungry and my mouth was watering, but I couldn't help thinking about what a guy that liked having things stuck up his butt could do with French fries.

"This is soooo good," Chameleon said.

I put on extra ketchup just in case, and ate them anyway.

A couple more days ahead was Quincy, the next town with a reliable grocery store. I was especially keen to get there because Monica had sent my mountaineering tent and sleeping bag to the post office in town. The food we had gotten at the gas station didn't seem to have the same horsepower packed into it as our usual staples so we spent most of the trail from Sierra City to Chester a little on the hungry side. I found myself thinking about meals I had eaten and actually remembering what it was that had been on my plate. This is very rare for me. Chameleon wondered aloud why more people didn't eat whipped cream on their pizzas, and speculated about what her friends' pets might taste like. Once at a lunch stop, I saw her collecting ants with a dollop of cake frosting on her finger and popping them into her mouth. "Hmm. I think this is my new favorite way to eat insects," she said. She was starting to scare me a little.

Just before we got into town, we saw another pair of PCT hikers- the first we saw other than ourselves for the last 260 miles. We had been mostly alone on the trail since we had left Independence and it was nice to see some other folks out walking for a change. It seemed that they had had the same idea that we did, skipping over the Sierras and coming back a bit later when the snow had a chance to melt off.

The Feather River Community College was graduating the 2018 class when we got into Quincy so there were no rooms to be had anywhere. A friendly couple sitting next to us in a pizza parlor overheard us working the phones unsuccessfully and offered to let us stay the night in a pop-up trailer in their driveway. I paid for their meal and we jumped at the chance as it was raining cats and dogs outside again.

The trailer was damp and unheated but a whole lot better than tenting in the rain again. We used their laundry and Wi-Fi and left the next morning to resupply again and hit the trail. Somewhere between the laundry in the garage and the pop-up trailer Chameleon picked up a couple of fleas to keep her company for the next section.

I was in heaven for this stretch, having a real sleeping bag and a waterproof tent and it got even better when the sun came out for good a couple days in. We took a long lunch break, exploded our packs and dried everything in the Sun. Chameleon was able to get the fleas shook out of her stuff.

When she's not walking, Chameleon is a pre-school teacher that specializes in early detection and therapy for autistic toddlers. My wife believes she probably has the ideal background for anyone forced to communicate with me.

"Now I am adding noodles to my hot water. I won't bring my water to a boil because I've already filtered it. This will conserve stove fuel. Now I am stirring it, putting the lid on it and setting it aside till it's ready to eat."

Her job with toddlers has accustomed her to narrate clearly everything she does as she's doing it. With me as her new audience, she hadn't seen the need to change.

"I am setting up my tent with four stakes. One stake goes in each corner because my tent is a square. This is my puffy jacket. I only wear this in camp. These are my night socks. I'm very careful to put them back on the same feet. My feet have big toes and they have little toes and they stretch the sock differently. I am putting my left sock onto my left foot. Now I am putting my right sock onto my right foot."

At first, I'd try to make some kind of reply- someone told me it was polite to be an active listener. But after a short while I gave it up and remained mute. Chameleon said that I reminded her a lot of her students at work.

Chameleon had hiked the Appalachian Trail two years earlier, and she taught me a lot about efficient long- distance hiking. She was a good human, and all in all a fantastic hiking partner.

Chameleon was an independent 29 years old, and had a devoted boyfriend in Ventura, California where she grew up in a middle class neighborhood. She was mostly through high school before she noticed that she was the only Hispanic there and it didn't bother her overly much. Then to college at Cal State Bakersfield, for a BS degree in early child development. From there, she went to a two square mile island in Micronesia for the Peace Corps, and in the two years she was there brought the school's test scores up from bottom place to third.

She also crossed two hundred miles of open ocean between islands on a dilapidated, unlicensed, and barely sea-worthy fishing boat that wallowed over swells at about six knots. She spent most of these crossings lying prone on the front deck, because she couldn't lift her head without puking. The guys would shoo the pigs they were transporting out of the way if they caught a Marlin, then gut and dress it on the deck beside her. When the boat shipped water over the decks, it washed fish guts and pig crap all over her. Still, she said, it was better than sitting up.

Chameleon's best friend at school was her cousin, who was born with cystic fibrosis. Just after Chameleon left for college, her cousin and best friend died.

Her mom developed mouth cancer and at first it seemed that it had been successfully treated with radiation. But then a sore developed on her jaw that wouldn't heal. After a couple years of salves, and hyperbaric chamber treatments, doctors realized that the radiation treatments had killed her jawbone's marrow and the bone was dead. They removed her jawbone and fashioned a new one of sorts from one of her fibulas (the smaller of the two lower leg bones) to rebuild her jaw. Today she's alive and well. The only thing she can't do is eat solid food.

Chameleon's older brother joined the Marines, fought two tours in Afghanistan, came home and married his high school sweetheart. Their future looked bright and soon they were expecting. They had a perfectly healthy baby girl, but there were complications during the delivery and in the next couple of days, things went terribly wrong. His wife went toxic, then into a coma and never came out.

His wife's parents had strong religious beliefs about medical treatments and fate. At their insistence, their daughter has been kept on life support. They remodeled a wing of their house into a medical facility and installed their vegetative daughter into it. They have every expectation that she will make a miraculous recovery at any time, and tell their granddaughter that "Mommy's going to wake up soon."

Her brother moved to Colorado to get enough distance to make a healthy environment to raise his daughter in. The grandparents have visitation rights to the girl, now five years old, and bring her back every month to visit her comatose mother. Her brother has remained single, legally and technically still married.

Chameleon moved to Colorado to help her brother raise his daughter, planning to stay there for the next couple years until her niece is older and emotionally able to understand the situation. And her brother. She figured that in another five years her niece and brother wouldn't need her anymore. She has informed her boyfriend that at that time he is expected to impregnate her.

"He isn't scared," said Chameleon.

He probably should be.

After we were thrown together in Kennedy Meadows, Chameleon and I hiked the rest of California with each other- about 1,000 miles. Two people that travel long distances together, on foot and stripped of everyday distractions, get to know each other fully- the good, the bad, the ugly, the wondrous, and the absurd. A friend told me that when two people spend a lot of time on the trail together, they invariably develop extreme feelings towards each other. That is, they will either love or loathe each other, with no area in between. Well, my friend is wrong. Chameleon and I didn't come to hate each other; and we weren't in love, either. What developed between us was a realistic mutual respect.

64

Nearing Chester we were definitely out of the Sierra and the country was looking more like home to me. We were just south of Mount Lassen, the southernmost of the Cascades volcanoes. From there north is a volcano up the chain every forty miles or so all the way up into British Columbia.

BEAR TREES AND SNORE WHACKERS

Miles on Trail... 897

Snow and rain were pretty much behind us now, and the miles rolled steadily out behind us. Sometimes we'd chat and hike together, but usually not. It's easier to walk your own personal gait than it is to constantly adjust your pace to another's. If we were walking together, I'd be in front. Chameleon didn't like people walking right behind her. It made her feel like she was being pushed, and I respected that. Except for one morning when a rattlesnake scared me. Greenish-colored, coiled, and rattling. He was right there within striking distance and as big around as my wrist. I don't like snake country and I don't like snakes. For the rest of that day, I kept Chameleon right in front of me.

We would break for lunch and eat together, plan a campsite ahead and either walk there together or meet up to camp. We developed an efficient camping routine. We'd agree on tent spots, and then I'd start a fire while she set her tent up and went inside. She would emerge, washed and changed into her camp clothes, to tend the fire and gather firewood for the night while I set up my tent and went inside to change. Then we'd do our laundry, usually rinsing and wringing out trail clothes at a nearby stream, and then dry them over the fire while we cooked and ate dinner. It took me longer to eat, getting everything down for the calories I needed for dinner, so Chameleon would finish first, brush her teeth, and go set up a bear tree.

A bear tree is a tree some distance from camp, with a good horizontal-ish branch from which you can hang a bag containing your food, cookset, toothpaste, and anything else that could be smelly, to keep safe from bears for the night. You need to toss a rope weighted with a rock or a stick over the branch, usually a good twenty feet up overhead. On the rare occasions when the task fell to me, I would usually tangle the rope in the wrong branch or the rock weight would come loose and fly off through the woods somewhere without taking the bear rope with it. Chameleon made it look a lot easier than it was. Being an early riser, it was my job to retrieve the food from the bear hang in the morning.

"The bear tree is on the other side of the creek back there tonight." she said. The last creek we had crossed was at least a quarter mile behind us.

"That's a long ways away," I said, puzzled. We were in the woods and there were lots of trees with branches all around us. "Was it hard to find a bear tree tonight?", I asked.

"Well I'm starting my special week," she explained, "and I want to be especially safe. That's why your tent is closer to the trail tonight. If a bear comes for me, he'll go to your tent first."

"Ah, the bait and switch gambit. It sort of makes sense. But what if the bear doesn't come waltzing up the trail but comes sniffing from over there instead?", I asked, pointing past her tent into the woods.

"Won't happen," she said. "I'm upwind of you."

"Bears aren't stupid. If there's a special scent that draws them in this far, they won't stop here at my tent and say 'Hey, this guy smells good enough. I think I'll eat him instead.' They'll still follow their nose right to your tent, you know."

"Well, what do you propose then?", she asked, irritated. "You won't be sleeping in this tent with me."

"Wouldn't want to, especially if you're sending out invitations for a bear party," I said. "You know, I don't think that bit of folklore is really true anyway. Bears won't be coming after you like sharks to blood, even if you are special this week. But you know, if you want to be perfectly safe I should probably sleep with all the food here and haul you up the bear tree tonight instead."

"Well, hah hah. Your jokes are so bad, it's hard telling when you're trying to be funny."

"I'm not trying to be funny, I'm serious. Well, sleep tight!"

Chameleon is afraid of bears, and is very circumspect in her camping practices and hygiene. Much more so than most other PCT hikers, whose attitudes generally ranged from cavalier to contemptuous. Two-Tents was one of these, and he camped with us for a night near Drakesbad.

"I'm not afraid of bears," he said. "They're nothing but a bunch of scavengers. If they want to get my food they'll have to go through me first because I am sleeping with it."

Two-Tents once spent a couple weeks on the trail with no shelter after misplacing his tent. "Shit happens," he shrugged when he told me about it. So now he carries two tents, for those occasions where he loses one. How do you lose a tent? It just doesn't seem possible. But he's lost several along his trek, enough so that now he only buys and carries cheap ones. I reflected upon the thought processes of a guy that loses tents as he continued talking about bears.

"Bears are way more scared of us than we are of them," he said. "Everyone knows that."

"Well, everyone says that," I said. "But that doesn't necessarily make it true."

"It's not true. And not everyone even says that," Chameleon pointed out.

My thoughts on bears are more in line with Chameleon's, and doubt that bears are especially motivated by a blind fear of humans. They're pretty smart.

"What are you laughing about?", asked Two-Tents.

"Oh, sorry. Two random synapses shorting out. You know how it gets on the trail," I said. But I couldn't help but smile. I was thinking about bears scattered along the trail behind us- comfortably sleeping in tents tonight, courtesy of the guy camped with us that night.

We were setting up camp one night when Chameleon said, "You have issues. When you sleep it sounds like someone stuffing hamsters one at a time down a garbage disposal- 'Akkk-SNORRRrrt-Squeak!' - 'Akkk-SNORRRrrt-Squeak!' - 'Akkk-SNORRRrrt-Squeak!'. I need to sleep and last night you kept me awake again."

"Really? It sounds like your issues. I've been sleeping pretty well lately," I said.

"I know. I was yelling and shining my flashlight at your tent all night. You kept right on snoring."

"Well, I could set my tent up farther away."

"What, in the next county? Because that's what it would take, and that's too far away."

"Hmm. This is a problem," I said, thinking.

I like problems. I'm an optimist that believes every problem is precious and pregnant with a beautiful solution. It just takes a little thought and ingenuity to bring about an immaculate birth. It's sort of a whimsical mysticism I indulge in quite often. Sometimes I think I was born too late because we live now in a world of convenience where most of our problems have already been solved, so I look to the elegant solutions all around us and contemplate the problems that necessitated their births. Like shopping carts, elegant. You can push one around a store with your groceries, take it out to your car, and then shove it into a compact train of them when you're finished. Shopping carts are elegant, perfect solutions- loved children of the problems that spawned them.

You can even carry your kid around in one, in the little seat fold-out. My guess is that shopping carts are involved in a lot of family planning. "Well, yes I want another child too, but not right away. We can't have another child until little Johnny is walking. There's only one seat in a shopping cart you know."

"Hello. Earth to Rick. What are you staring at?" Chameleon had her hands on her hips.

"I'm thinking. Lookie here. There's a bunch of things I'm packing that don't get used at night, like these carabiners and trekking poles. We've been hanging all our food from your rope at night, so I've got some eighty feet of para-chord we can use. Let's see, we can run the line from my tent to yours. When I snore, you pull- "

"-and the other end is tied to your wrist. I pull the rope, you punch yourself in the face!" Chameleon said.

"I don't think that would work."

"Or I could just keep pulling, drag you out of your tent and across the ground."

"Well let's look at everything we have available here, like these carabiners and trekking poles. I was thinking I could suspend a trekking pole from the center of my tent, clip a water bottle to it, and then run the line through the carabiners like so out of my tent fly and into yours. You pull the line, the trekking pole swings around, and the water bottle whacks the side of my head."

Chameleon looked over the materials I had laid out. Resourcefulness is the art of solving problems using the resources you have at hand, and Chameleon was getting into the spirit of it. "Hmm," she said. "I've been packing a set micro-spikes. Let's attach them spikes out to the water bottle with my hair scrunchies. That would make more of an impression on you, don't you think?"

For the rest of California, I assembled the Snore-Whacker contraption in my tent every night. It wasn't exactly what anyone would call beautiful or elegant- as children of problems go it was more the 'problem child' type. But I had helped give it birth, so I was proud of it and only momentarily annoyed each time it worked.

TOSSING SHADE

Miles on Trail... 945

Coming out of the Mount Lassen Wilderness near Old Station we came into cell reception, and Chameleon learned that her brother had re-married. She was beaming. Her brother was a good man, a good father, had endured unimaginable heartache, and deserved a good break from life. He deserved to be in love. Chameleon was proud of him for moving on, and ecstatic for him.

He and his new bride had once been high school sweethearts. But when he had gone into the Marines and off to Afghanistan, she had married one of her brother's friends. Life happened, she had four children, divorced and found herself a single mom. To make room, Chameleon's brother and his new wife had moved Chameleon's belongings out of her room and crammed them into her car. The townhouse was still too small. Combined, they had five children and were looking for a new place to make room for the family of seven. I asked Chameleon where she would live when she was done with the trail.

"Well, I'm not going back to California," she said. "I told my boyfriend that our plans will be moving up. I don't need to take care of my brother and niece now, but I'm going to stay in Colorado. He's agreed to come out and try living there with me for a couple years. I told him to start looking for a place to build a tiny house."

I wondered how difficult it would be for her boyfriend to pack up and move. "What does your boyfriend do for a living? Will it be a problem for him to transfer to Colorado or will he have to find a new job?", I asked.

"Oh, it'll be easy," Chameleon said. "He doesn't have a job officially. He lives with his parents and helps his mom and dad with things around the house doing chores and things."

"Uh, how old is he?" I asked.

"He's twenty-nine, like me," she said. "He was going to Community College for Environmental Studies, but he didn't like it and dropped out. He's doing some night classes now."

"Well, what does he do for money?" I asked.

"Oh, he's good with money. He's saved a lot and is very careful with it. He has money. Whenever we go out, he pays."

"It's good that he's careful with money," I said. "But if he's not getting a paycheck, how does he get the money to start with?"

"People give him money," Chameleon said.

"Why? Who gives him money?"

"You know, family. Birthdays, Christmas, things like that. He's an only child and has a good-sized extended family that gives him money. And he's been careful with it."

We walked without talking for a bit, and I wondered how that would work. There are birthdays, and Christmas; that's two paydays a year. Maybe Easter, so that would be three. He could be getting a payday every four months or so. If he lives rent free, and gets free groceries that would probably be enough, I thought. I used to get paid for each A on my report card, and wondered if he had. Probably not I decided, or he wouldn't have dropped out.

I wondered if as he got older he found more money enclosed in his birthday cards. I hoped so, because as time went on, there would be a tendency for the extended family's older members to die off. You know, so that over time he'd be getting fewer birthday cards. But at twenty-nine, maybe there hadn't been many deaths in his family yet.

But still, I thought, he must have gotten used to living with at least one pay cut. At his age, the Tooth Fairy wasn't coming anymore. Unless-

"Hey, does your boyfriend have all his teeth?", I asked.

"What kind of question is that? Of course he does." I could hear her pack rustle as she quickened up a bit to get closer behind me. "I know what you're thinking, "she said. "And he's not lazy. Since he's quit school he's started classes two nights a week at the community college."

"What kind of classes?"

"Improvisational performance classes. And he's good at it. Also, he runs errands and goes grocery shopping for his folks sometimes. Also, he cooks," she said. "He's a great cook."

"Well, I'm not judging or saying anything about that," I said. "When I was his age, I was working my ass off, owned a dairy farm and herd of cows, and had plans to make a pile of money and live my dream. But it turned out to be a pretty dumb idea. So who am I to say what a guy should be doing with his life?

"But I do know that it takes money to buy a house, even a tiny house. It would be tough to do on a pre-school teacher's salary. And it takes money to live. And if you want to have a baby and raise a child, it's a lot easier to do it with money than without. So one of you is going to have to make some."

Chameleon was quiet for a minute. Then she said, "I choose to not discuss this with you."

I've re-run in my mind that conversation often, and have regretted it anew every time. I'm such a dick sometimes, and I know it. After the fact, that is. If only I could realize that I am a dick while I am actually being one. I can imagine a really useful gadget, a dick detector, that would be worn on an earlobe and look exactly like a diamond stud. Whenever it heard me talking like a dick, it would heat up and burn my ear. 'Ouch,' I'd think. "I should quit being a dick.' But I don't know how to make one.

Of course Chameleon knew she'd need her boyfriend to contribute in a meaningful way if they were to start a life together. But there would be time to worry about it later. Right then, it was time to celebrate and to be happy for her brother. And I cut that time short, cheated her. "Tossing shade," as Chameleon would say.

I'm always thinking of what the next thing is, and how to do that, and then the next thing and how to do that. I'm not half-bad as a planner or doer, but at dreaming and celebrating I'm pretty deficient. And life is just too short to squander opportunities for celebrations. I don't mean to be a shade-tosser, but when my mind follows its natural thought processes I toss shade all around before I even know I'm doing it.

If anyone invents a dick detector, I'll buy it. I'll be its first customer.

We were still in a subdued state of mind when we came to the Subway Caves picnic area later that same day. There were a couple lava tube caves there to explore, but the most striking looked for all the world like a subway tunnel. Lava tubes are formed during volcanic eruptions when flows of hot lava slowly cool as they ooze downhill. Lava is actually rock that is so hot that it's melted into a molten form, sort of like toothpaste. When lava cools off a bit, it turns back into rock.

In a lava flow its outermost edges will naturally cool off before its center. It's simple physics. If you've ever been impatient and tried to eat a corndog before it's cooled enough, you've already tested this yourself. Even when the outside of a corndog has cooled enough to touch, it's insides are still hot enough to burn the bejeebers out of your mouth. Lava tubes are like hollow corndogs, where the 'dog' parts of them flowed out before they cooled.

Alright, I'll admit that my understanding of geomorphology is less than comprehensive. Actually, lava tubes are not hollow corndogs. They are hollow mozzarella sticks. Anyway, if the conditions are right when they form, lava tubes can be impressively large. And conditions were right some 24,000 years ago during one of Mount Lassen's eruptions. The main Subway Cave is more than twenty feet in diameter and a quarter mile long. Its walls and arching roof are impressively smooth, as if a team of finish plasterers had worked them. The floor isn't as smooth, but is level and relatively easy to walk on.

The cave, being just a bit underground and out of the weather, stays constantly at the area's average temperature of forty-six degrees. That was informative. On the day we were there it was some eighty-four degrees outside, so Hat Creek must get pretty cold in the winter. It was also dark in there, completely dark, like the inside of a cow dark. We had brought the little led headlamps we used inside our tents with us, but they were too feeble to do much more than, well, illuminate the inside of a tent. There inside the Subway Cave, they were laughable.

There were water spigots scattered amongst the picnic tables outside, so Chameleon and I washed our feet, rinsed and wrung our socks, and draped them over some tree branches to dry while we ate lunch. We didn't look at each other or talk much, neither of us being happy with the morning's conversation.

Two overweight retired couples were at the picnic table adjacent to us, so we watched and listened to them instead. They hadn't used parking spaces, but had pulled their trucks off the pavement nearly on top to their picnic table so they could keep their walking to a minimum. The guys carried a cooler to the picnic table from one of the trucks. Their job evidently done, they squished their bellies into the picnic table across from each other and watched as their wives waddled several trips between table and trucks. Two jumbo buckets of Kentucky Fried Chicken, mashed potatoes and gravy, four family-size bags of potato chips, Walmart-sized Oreos and Chips Ahoys. There was no way they could eat all of it.

But they could, and they did. We stared dumbly, transfixed by their mindless gluttony. It was disgustingly fascinating. They consumed it all with a relaxed, well-practice ease, transferring food from plates to mouths with both hands. They talked inanely with mouths full, rolling boluses of half-chewed food to one cheek or other when it was their turn to talk. Their napkins held chunks and dribbles they had wiped off their faces, food enough for two days on the PCT.

Their conversation was smug and self-satisfied, rotating roles but conforming to a single simple pattern. One of them would mention an event. The next two would add color commentary, as if they were Fox News contributors, and the third would offer a solution.

"They're opening a Starbucks in town." *Munch Munch.*

"Free trade coffee? That's stupid." *Munch munch.*

"Give me a break." "Probably be all 'politically correct'," *Munch* "try to make a sanctuary for illegals."

"Yeah." *Munch munch* "Should toss all of 'em back over the wall."

Whatever event they started with, the solution usually involved a wall, either for tossing someone over or for lining them up against to be shot.

I looked at Chameleon and wondered what she thought. Chameleon had already told me that the word 'illegals' isn't in most people's vocabularies. And when there are people around that do use the word, what they mean when they say it is 'Hispanics'. She had been two years in the Peace Corps and her brother had fought two tours in Afghanistan. Were they 'illegals' to 'toss back over the wall'?

As they talked and ate, I wondered how it happened. Was there some trauma that suddenly forced them into a bigoted worldview to survive, or were they responding to a gradual realization that their lives were lived without purpose? "I'm over-thinking this," I thought. "It's probably gout."

"Hey Chameleon," I said. "I hope we're friends for a long time, and I want you to promise me something."

"What?"

"If I ever get like that, no matter how many years in the future," I said, nodding towards the other picnic table, "I want you to kill me. Promise."

Chameleon thought about it. "No," she said, looked over towards the other picnic table, then back to me. "It's just not worth it."

There would be no water source for the next thirty miles of trail so we left the picnic area with all the water we could carry. It wasn't so bad as it turned out, we were pretty early in the season yet and just a half mile to the west, found several shallow ponds along a forest service road that paralleled the trail. Smallish, orange winged butterflies ringed the ponds, settled on the mud wings flapping slowly. I don't know what they were doing or why, but it was fascinating to watch. The bands were about four feet wide and they had spaced themselves wingtip to wingtip. From a distance, it looked like someone had bordered the ponds with a giant orange highlighter.

To get to the water we moved slowly, careful not to stomp on any. As we did, all the butterflies within about arm's reach would lift and flutter about, giving us both our own personal Oort cloud, made up of hundreds of little individual spirit-lifters. This, I think, is my favorite mode of travel.

A few days later we got a ride in to Burney from Brian, on his way to the laundromat. A couple trash bags of clothes were up in the cab with us. In back of the truck were more trash bags, these filled with trash. Interspersed among them were soiled grease rags and empty Skoal tins. There was a big highway widening project nearby and Brian had landed a job as the night greaser. There was a lot of heavy equipment on the job working sun up to sun down, and each night it was Brian's job to refuel and lubricate them all. He worked alone wearing a headlamp and it took him all night.

Brian's truck smelled like diesel fuel. There was axle grease on the steering wheel, radio knobs, blinker lever, gear shift, door handles, on the inside of the windshield, on the seat, and on the roof. Pretty much everywhere. Brian himself smelled like diesel fuel and was smeared liberally with axle grease as well. He unfastened a child's seat and put it on top of the laundry bags to make room for us. Chameleon trusted him immediately and slid into the cab first, seating herself between us. Usually, she would position me there.

"I like the smell of heavy equipment," I said. "It smells like things getting done."

"Yeah. I like the smell of it too," Brian said. "It's a cool job. I get to drive everything and move things around so I can get to all the zerk fittings. It's important to grease all of them, with equipment that big. There's a couple 800 excavators there."

"It looks like hard work," Chameleon said.

"It is. But it's a good job, and the money is okay. Only problem is the laundry. I'm living with my mom right now and she doesn't want my work clothes going in her washing machine. That's why I'm heading in to town to the laundromat."

"So do you have a kid," I asked, nodding towards the child's seat balanced behind us.

"Yep, a two-year-old daughter. She's great. Right now I'm sort of a single parent so my mom is helping out, letting us live there and things. It's not too bad."

Brian worked alone on night shifts, and spent almost every other waking hour with his two year-old daughter. Conversing with people wasn't something he could do much of.

"My wife and I used to party a lot. And drugs. We got high together a lot and it was okay, you know it didn't seem to matter really. And then she got pregnant and Alexis came along. She was beautiful, healthy and everything. Like a miracle or something, because we were getting high the whole time before she was born.

"So we were like, 'we've got to get clean and be parents now with this baby' and so we cleaned up our acts, quit the drugs. It was hard, but it was worth it and I thought we were going to do the family thing. The three of us, you know. But my wife missed partying too much and getting high so she got herself a boyfriend to do drugs with. I came home from work one morning, and Alexa was wandering around outside with her diapers full and my wife and her boyfriend wasted on the floor.

"Now we live with my mom. Whenever I see my wife, she says she'll quit drugs and cries and promises and everything. And she means it too, but she just can't. I don't think she ever will. It's not much, but I just want Alexa to grow up without drugs around, you know."

He peered through the windshield, looking out at the road that lay before him.

"Alexa is lucky to have you," Chameleon said. "You're a good human."

"You think so?" Brian asked.

"Absolutely."

LITTERBUGS AND CREEPERS

Miles on Trail... 997

The Scott Mountain campground is halfway between Etna and Weaverville on Highway 3 where the PCT crosses it. There were no water faucets there but it was a nice campground, clean and well laid out.

But one of the campsites was trashed. Someone had opened and gone through a flat-rate mailing box, the kind that PCT hikers use to send ahead food and supplies to themselves, and left their unwanted detritus behind in one of the camp's fire rings. Squirrels and birds had held a yard sale with it; Ziploc bags, packets of Starbucks Via, Whole Foods powdered soup mixes, some kind of dried seaweed stuff, oatmeal and bullion cubes, section maps, and shredded toilet paper was scattered in a wide circle surrounding the fire ring. The hikers had left some Larrabars behind as well, but these were undisturbed. Even animals won't touch those things.

Whoever did it had carefully ripped the mailing and return addresses off the box everything had been mailed in.

"I'm going to find out who did this. It can't be through hikers," Chameleon said. "They wouldn't do this." The box had been mailed from Tumwater, Washington. She took photos of the postmark, a wide shot of the trashed campsite, and close-ups of the bullion cubes and soup mixes.

"This soup mix isn't common. I'm pretty sure I'll get them."

"How's that?" I asked.

"I'm going to post this. See the maps they left behind? Those maps cover territory we've just hiked; they're done with those maps and heading north. I'll post these pictures on social media when we get back into cell range. There's a lot of people hiking south through here now, and I'll have them on the lookout."

"On the lookout for who? I mean what would they look for? We don't know anything about them."

"There's two of them. And they share meals. See? The soup mix has been portioned out into Ziplocs for single meals, and there's enough for two of them."

"So you'll have folks on the lookout for a pair of PCT hikers that share soup at night?" I asked.

"A pair of *section* hikers that share soup at night. Through-hikers wouldn't be eating a lot of this food, and by this stage of the game through-hikers know exactly how much they need to eat. They wouldn't have sent themselves this much extra. They're section hikers, and not very experienced ones."

"Hmm. 'Wanted. Be on lookout for two inexperienced northbound section hikers, possibly from Tumwater, that eat Whole Foods soup and drink Starbucks Via together.' You're going to post something like that?"

"Yep. And the photos. They'll be caught, no doubt."

"Maybe. I don't know," I said.

"I know. Down south, before you got on the trail, there were a couple of guys crapping in tent sites, right in the middle where you're supposed to set your tent up. No one ever saw them doing it, and the only evidence they left behind was fresh turds. People posted pictures and they got caught."

"So people posted poopy pictures?" I asked. The phrase tickled my brain when I heard myself say it, and Chameleon waited a moment as I compulsively whispered it to myself a couple times. "So people posted poopy pictures.. So people posted poopy pictures"

"Well, was that good?" she asked.

"Just so-so."

"So yes, people posted poopy pictures. And"-

"Was it their duty, would you say?"

"No, but you would. And the hiking community compared notes online; everyone was on the lookout, figuring out the guys' mileage and hiking speed. It didn't take too long before they were pinpointed and outed on social media. They confessed, apologized, and then quit the trail and went home."

I tried to imagine what would happen online when Chameleon posted the pictures. "You may be right," I said. "You could very well find out who did this."

"I'll find them." Chameleon was confident, Sherlock Holmes confident. But where Sherlock cast his web with newspaper personals and his gang of street urchins, Chameleon had hundreds of eyes on the trail, feeding and fed by a vitriolic internet.

There were no dumpsters or trash cans at the Scott Mountain campground, and it just wasn't possible to carry other people's trash with us for the next forty miles. So we put it all back into the fire pit and burned it.

There was one other guy tenting in the campground that night, but he hadn't seen anyone. He said that a Trail Angel had dropped him off there around noon and the trash was already spread out all over the place when he had gotten there. His tent was tilted, the fly saggy and inexpertly guyed to a couple of nearby trees. Clothing and camping gear were draped over or clipped to the guy lines. All of his gear was new.

He had set out from Campo to hike the PCT in April he said, but after a week on the trail and getting blisters had quit and gone back home to heal. He stayed home for four months. Now he was back on the trail and planned to hike north from here.

"So what are you doing different this time so you don't get blisters?" I asked.

"Well I'm here. I got those blisters hiking in the desert. It was brutal. So I'm not doing any desert any more," he said.

"Uh, I meant like shoes or socks or something. Are you going it with different shoes or socks this time?"

"Naw. Nothing wrong with these. It was the desert. Made my feet sweaty, you know."

Chameleon gave me a look, and without a word, moved her tent to the other side of the campsite and disappeared inside it. 'Great,' I thought. 'Now I have to re-rig the snore-whacker.'

The next morning I retrieved our food from the bear hang as usual, left Chameleon's food bag and parachord outside her tent fly, disassembled the snore-whacker, packed up, and left. I was only a half mile up the trail when Chameleon caught up to me, panting.

"Why did you leave me back there alone with that guy?" she asked.

"You mean the numb-nuts? Why?"

"Because that 'numb-nuts' is a serial rapist or murderer or something, that's why."

"He is? He told me he's an accountant."

"There's something not right about that guy. Why do you think I moved my tent last night? And I gave you a look. Why do you think I did that, huh?"

I thought about it. "Well for the same reason you always do things," I answered.

"And what's that?"

"No freakin' idea."

"Well he's going to try catching up with us. With me, anyway. When I left he was cramming things into his pack like nobody's business. I'm telling you, that guy's a creeper. He's out here alone, starting his hike here in the middle of nowhere where nobody starts a hike, and he's got all new gear that he doesn't even know how to use. Did you see him trying to cook?"

"No, not really," I said.

"He doesn't even know how to boil a hotdog. When I saw that, I knew he was evil. That's why I moved my tent to the other side of yours."

I had never considered hotdog boiling technique to be the least bit consequential before. But here's the thing- female primates have always been physically outmatched by males. They have always had to quickly, intuitively, assess their counterparts' intentions. "Will this male assault or protect me?" Women have some seven million years of Darwinian pressure informing their intuition. It's powerful, and not to be dismissed.

"Okay," I said.

"Okay," said Chameleon. "He's going to try catching us, and we need to stay close together today, okay? No running off and daydreaming. I want to see you all day."

"Okay"

Sure enough, the guy caught up to us at a stream crossing while we were refilling our water bottles. He'd been trotting, and was streaming sweat from wearing too many clothes. His hat was hanging over his chest from tie strings around his neck, his shoulder straps were uneven, and his backpack listed to one side. Camping gear was attached to it and hanging from it awkwardly. His dinner pot and toilet trowel were clipped to the same carabiner.

Chameleon gave me the look again (*'Now I know what it means,'* I thought) and quickly topped off her water. She got back on the trail in front of me.

"Hey, where are you guys camping tonight?" he asked.

He had taken off his backpack and was leaning over the stream, hands on his knees and looking up at me. His face wore the same crooked grin, but it looked somehow different this time.

"We're not going very far," I told him. "There's a good campsite eleven miles up the trail. We'll see you there," I told him.

We never saw him again. Chameleon set a brisk pace and we made twenty-three miles that day, and got in to Etna the next.

WHAT HAPPENS ONLINE

Miles on Trail... 1,052

We stayed in the Hiker Hut in Etna. It was an outbuilding to a beautiful old estate house that had started life as a three stall horse barn but had been converted to a hostel-style lodging for PCT hikers. In it was everything a hiker missed on the trail; a flushing toilet, a shower, refrigerator, a hot plate, and a microwave oven. It was clean and cheerily appointed, with flags from countries all over the world hanging from the rafters and vaulted ceilings. The hosts were great, they ran a bed and breakfast in the main house and were good with taking care of their guests. They couldn't have made much money off us PCT'ers, but they treated us kindly and almost protectively. There was a shelf of men's and women's used clothing so we could do our laundry there, in a cantankerous old washing machine in what used to be the root cellar under the main house. Wiring and plumbing hung loosely below open floor joists overhead to feed the washer. There were extra joints in the pipes; it looked like it had they had frozen and burst a couple times.

There were two sets of bunkbeds in the hut, four beds in all, and the bottom bunks were already taken. A mother-son pair of section hikers had gotten in the day before us. The mom was there, but the son part of the duo had gone to the post office to retrieve this trip's last resupply box. She cleared their extra things off the top bunks for us. I wasn't enthusiastic. The last time I'd stayed in a hostel's upper bunk, I'd been gassed out at two in the morning and had been forced outside for the final performance of a poorly-tuned ukulele. I hoped these two weren't eating pork 'n beans at least.

Chameleon seemed happy to have someone new to chat with, and was getting their life story from the woman. She had been a young single mom and had raised her son single-handedly. She sold figurines to tourists in Arizona at a roadside table under a shade tarp. Every day that she worked, she took her son with her and they did home schooling together beside the highway. When he was five he started playing a ukulele, busking for people that stopped at their table.

"You wouldn't believe the rude things people would say to a child," she said. "'Don't give the little money-grubber anything', they'd say. 'You play terribly!' 'Everyone hates ukuleles!' they'd say. And he was just a little boy."

That reminded me again of the last ukulele I'd listened to. I grimaced, and wondered at the lack of empathy I felt for them. 'I'm only human,' I decided.

They scrabbled out a living at a roadside table, being ignored and passed by at fifty miles an hour by my most, and ridiculed by some, and haggled with by others for eighteen years. They painted and sold a lot of porcelain tortoises and burros. It was an odd life, and one that affirmed for them both that out of all the people in all the world, the only ones they could place their faith in was each other.

I thought she had some weird loaner clothes on to do her laundry, but it turned out that she wore a dark blue Hawaiian flower print muumuu that covered her ankles out on the trail. It was her favorite thing to hike in. The two of them hiked a hundred miles of trail together every year and they were halfway through this year's hike, their tenth. This was a special hike, because after this one their lives would change. He was going off to college, and they would live apart for the first time since he had been born.

Her son came back from the post office. He was cheerful and friendly, slightly pudgy, and less tanned than you'd expect from someone that had been outdoors in Arizona for much of his life. He had soft looking skin on his cheeks and arms. He had come back from the post office with a flat rate shipping box under his arm. He put it on the small table and cut it open with his pocket knife. Inside, we're Ziploc bags of Whole Foods soup mix and Starbucks Via coffee packets.

Chameleon and I looked at each other. She continued to chat with the pair amiably while they repacked their backpacks and food bags for the next section. They were leaving to get back onto the trail the next day and would be busy re-organizing gear and catching up with Facebook posts for the rest of the evening. Chameleon and I left them to it and borrowed a couple bicycles from the house for the three-quarter mile ride into town. For some reason, Chameleon wanted a salad this time. As usual for my first meal in a town, I ordered a hamburger and a beer.

"That's them," Chameleon said. "I told you we would find them."

"So what are we going to do now?" I asked. "Are you going to tell them that we found all their trash? Are you going to tell them that we've been picking up after them?", I asked.

"No, not yet," Chameleon said. "I don't have enough yet."

"Enough? Enough what?" I asked. "What more do you need?"

"I need proof, real proof. I need pictures."

"You're going to take their pictures?", I asked.

"I don't need pictures of them. When they leave tomorrow morning, you are going to go through the trash and take pictures of that box", she said.

"Why me? Why don't you do it?"

She rolled her eyes. "Because," she said, "I'm not going to do it. You are."

So the next morning after waving the pair off, I went out to the dumpster behind the B & B. Looking around first to see if anyone was watching, I leaned inside and started rummaging around in the garbage. It didn't take long to find the box, and I looked around again to make sure no one was watching as I got my phone out. Even though I had lain awake fabricating cover stories all night, I still didn't have a reasonable one to explain why I would be taking pictures of garbage. I didn't want to be caught.

No one around. Quickly I took some pictures, then stood up, closed the dumpster's lid, and walked off nonchalantly. I reviewed the pictures on my phone. There were names addressed on this box, both to and from. And not trail names, either. Real names. I sent Chameleon the photos, then walked on into town.

There was a bench outside the town's library, under a flowery trellis attended by honeybees. I sat and called home. Monica and Matthew were both there at home, and seeing them on screen made my eyes well up again. They were looking forward to the end of school, and meeting up with me in Tahoe, not too far off now. I felt like a cactus in a rain shower as their conversation pattered over me.

My phone had been chiming text notifications as we talked so after the call home I checked them out. Chameleon had found the litterbugs' Facebook pages. They had posted pictures of themselves hiking together, comments, itinerary, and campsites. One of their posts thanked the lady's sister, who lived in Tumwater, and was sending them resupply boxes of groceries from Whole Foods.

She had also sent me a link to the PCT hikers discussion board. Chameleon had posted pictures of the trashed campsites to the discussion board only the night before, and it had already unleashed a shitstorm of vituperation. It's incredible what people with online personas like 'Butterfly Dancer' or 'Quick Bunny' will advocate doing to people that hadn't done much more than leave toilet paper out in the woods. And now Chameleon had pictures of the litterbugs, their names, and their itinerary. If Chameleon decided to out them on the internet, they were dead meat.

Chameleon and I had started on the PCT rather on the early side, so we were some of the first hikers into the Sierras when we were met with too much snow to pass through. Remember, we had bussed around the Sierras then, 350 miles to Donner Pass before resuming northbound on the PCT. Our plan was to hike to Ashland, get a rental car and drive it back to Donner Pass, and then hike from there south through the Sierra. Chameleon and a handful of other early hikers had been posting updates of the snow and weather conditions all along the way. The PCT hikers behind us had learned from our experience, and the main body of them had skipped not only the Sierras, but also the wet and sloggy portions we had just finished with. They left the trail south of where we did, at Lake Isabella, and from there bussed north all the way to Ashland, Oregon. They were getting back on the trail there and heading south, towards us.

Each day in the section ahead, we would pass dozens of these southbound PCT hikers coming down the trail. The litterbugs would as well. If Chameleon outed them, if she posted links to their Facebook pages now, they would be recognized by everyone they met the trail. It would be like walking through a buzzsaw.

I went to the bakery for breakfast, light reading, and some local color and went back to the Hiker Hut. Today was a zero-day, a rest up and resupply day.

"I'm not going to out them just yet.," Chameleon said when I got back. "From their posts, I know how far they hike each day and where they are going. If we just hike our normal hike, we'll catch up to them in a couple of days and I'll talk with them first."

Chameleon was happy being back on the trail and looking forward to seeing some old friends. Before she had met Cool Breeze and me, she had hiked 300 miles with a group she thought of as her first PCT family. She liked and got along with them well, but they weren't making the daily mileage she needed. They were also in the southbound contingent ahead of us, hiking down the trail towards us now.

"Boy, will they be surprised to see me hiking with you," Chameleon said. "They would never have guessed that I would be hiking with one of the Grumpy Old Men."

"One of the whats?" I asked.

"One of the Grumpy Old Men," Chameleon said. "You know, you and Cool Breeze."

"No, I don't know me and Cool Breeze", I said.

"Well, that's what everyone on Facebook called you guys. I thought you knew."

"No I didn't know, I don't do Facebook. And Cool Breeze doesn't even have a cell phone," I said. "And besides, that's not fair. I'm not grumpy. Since I've started this hike, I haven't been grumpy. Not at all."

"What about Bird Pass."

"Bird Pass? Where's that?"

"Bird Pass. You know. There was a water cache there, south of Lake Isabella and Walker Pass. Blue Dog said you were grumpy there. You and Cool Breeze got there and all the tent sites were already taken. He'd been there a while and was trying to be helpful and showed you where you could put your tent and you were rude to him. Both of you were. He called you two the Grumpy Old Men when he posted about it, and that's what you guys were called ever since."

"Really? He was strutting around there like he owned the place and talking on his cell phone, like really loud and bragging about stuff. We were refilling our water bags and he came over and told us where we had to camp."

"And then you were rude to him."

"He pointed at a snafflehound midden behind the water cache and said, 'You need to camp there'. And I said 'No, I don't.'"

"And then you asked who made him God, right?"

"Well no, but Cool Breeze did. I just pointed down the hill a ways and said we could camp over there, and he said no we couldn't. There were cows over there. I like cows, I spent half my life on a dairy farm, you know? But he didn't seem like the kind of guy that could let a conversation drop if you disagreed with him, so I just shrugged and left."

"He said you set up your tent where everyone else was crapping."

"So everyone there was crapping out in the open, in full view of the other tents? I don't think so."

"Well that's what he said. He posted it online and it got a lot of comments."

"So this Blue Dog guy, is he on the trail now coming towards us?"

"No. He quit the trail at Walker Pass."

Apparently, he had quit the trail just after I had seen him. His posts about me and Cool Breeze must have been his parting shots.

"That's too bad," I said. "Old Blue Dog is missing an opportunity to meet a real grumpy old man."

I was determined after that to be extra cheerful and chatty with all the hikers we met. A few of them were familiar, acquaintances that I had somehow passed on the trail far back in Southern California. The hikers that recognized me called me either JR or Finn, depending upon just where we had last seen each other. And for the hikers that didn't recognize me, none of them referred to me as one the grumpy old men. At one point, Chameleon stopped and hugged a woman wearing a flower print skirt over gray leggings. She had long wavy hair, and grayish blue eyes over wide cheekbones in a smiling face. Her name was Kitty and she was hiking with her husband, Shoeless. Shoeless got his name because he hiked everywhere in leather sandals. He had a leather thong string with a little Mojo bag tied to it around his neck, and was wearing a leather kilt over dirty and mud splattered legs. He was short and sinewy, and looked like the kind of guy that could run straight through a wall. He was smiling too.

Kitty and Shoeless were Chameleon's first PCT family, and they were happy to see each other again. Kitty and Shoeless don't make a lot of miles each day, and they're not in hurry to get anywhere either. If the weather turned before the trail was done, they would just go to the other end of it or somewhere else together. They had been apart while Shoeless served multiple tours of duty in Iraq. And things happened to him over there that now made living in and around buildings difficult for him. When he came back, he couldn't sleep under a roof or even use the kitchen in his own home. When Kitty was faced with a choice of living in a house or living with her man, there was no hesitation. They have been together hiking almost nonstop ever since. They get by on his military pension and disability income, living outdoors and walking trails. They have walked, by their estimate, somewhere around 12,000 miles together. They don't make a big fuss about it, it's just what they do.

I thought again about DJ, and hoped he was sleeping well. If he was still on the trail I should be seeing him again in this section. But I didn't.

Just about where and when Chameleon had predicted we'd overtake the Litterbugs, we did. I came around a corner of the trail, and there up ahead, was a dark blue muumuu wearing a backpack. I stopped and waited, and when Chameleon saw them up ahead, continued on straightaway. It didn't take her long to overtake them.

They looked back when they heard us behind them, and then stepped to the side at a wide spot on the trail. It seemed like they had been expecting us, and waited there for us to speak first. Chameleon and the woman talked, while her son and I just stood there listening, uncomfortably mute. They had seen the pictures of the trashed campsites that Chameleon had posted and the awful comments people had posted about them. They hadn't left the campsites that way, but had put their trash neatly in the fire rings. They had no idea that squirrels and jays would spread it all over the way they did. They loved the earth and the environment, and would never do anything knowingly to injure it. They didn't burn their trash because the ground was dry, and they were deathly afraid of starting a forest fire. The woman in the muumuu was crying.

Chameleon told her that she knew their names and had seen their Facebook pages. But whether or not she would out them by posting links, she hadn't decided yet. The woman cried harder, tears running down her cheeks unchecked. It was hard to watch so I turned away. Chameleon was unphased by the outburst, unembarrassed by the power she held over her. She faced the woman unmoved, hands on hips, deciding the woman's fate.

The woman pleaded with Chameleon not to post. She didn't fear the comments on the discussion board, or even meeting up with the commenters out here on the trail. She and her son had faced a lifetime of verbal abuse from strangers. But linking to her Facebook page, and breaching her circle of friends and family would be devastating. This was a special hike, a milepost between two chapters in their lives. All of their friends and family were sharing the experience, following and encouraging them online.

They had been packing of all their trash with them ever since they had left Etna, after they had seen Chameleon's photos. They would never leave anything behind ever again, anywhere. They were aghast when they saw what the animals did with the trash they had left behind. Their intent, putting a rock over it in a fire ring, was to leave a ready source of kindling for any hiker that came through later in the fall when it was colder and wetter.

She stopped talking and stood there, cheeks wet, arms limp at her sides. The two women stood looking at each other a long moment.

"Okay. I won't post, Chameleon said.

"Thank you," the woman said, almost whispered.

I followed Chameleon and when I looked back, saw that the mother and son weren't following us. They had taken off their backpacks and were sitting on them, facing each other and talking across the trail they were walking together. It occurred to me that I was witness to something important, the two of them processing an event that would remain unforgotten their entire lives.

In camp that night, Chameleon asked me if I thought the woman was sincere or had been putting on an act. She had been left with the impression that the woman was accustomed to getting away with things if only she'd put on an act that was convincing enough.

"I don't think she was acting," I said. "It's been my experience that people aren't as convincing as actors as they think they are."

"My experience is just the opposite. That people think they are better at spotting actors than they really are. I think we get duped more than we think," she said.

"I'd like to think you're wrong there," I said.

"Yeah. Well, I'd like to think that too," she said.

STATE OF JEFFERSON

Miles on Trail... 1,070

I'd first seen the seal of the independent State of Jefferson on a round plaque centered over a two-car garage door 300 miles back in Chester. It was in a pleasant neighborhood, the house was neatly painted and trimmed, and the yard was meticulously maintained; the lawn lushly green, weed-free and perfectly mowed. There was a mulched flower bed behind a white picket fence, precisely bordered, where bright flowers were growing, perfectly spaced. It was the nicest yard on the block. Whoever owned it had lavished more time, effort, and chemicals on his yard than anyone else in the neighborhood. It was obvious that whoever owned it cared a lot about how it looked. Nothing was out of place. And there in a place of pride was the green circle, proclaiming the independent State of Jefferson. I wondered in passing, and speculated about the person that had put it there. But it was an oddity, and as I didn't see any more plaques in the town let it drop from my mind.

In Etna, some of the vehicles and windows sported Trump-Pence and Make America Great Again bumper stickers and banners. And most of these shared space with State of Jefferson seals. The Jefferson seals weren't pasted only on private cars or residences either, but were also on some of the front windows on Main Street. There was one on the window of a bakery. It was early morning, the place was open so I went in.

There were a handful of customers inside, men mostly roughly dressed and on their way to work or pot-bellied and retired. All of them, working or retired wore baseball caps from tractor sales lots or American Legion outposts. They were all talking loudly. There was one woman customer, wearing a yoga outfit and running shoes that was sipping coffee, silently engrossed by something on her cell phone.

There were two women behind the counter making espressos and heating pastries. One woman was in her twenties, the other middle-aged. The younger woman had obviously worked there longer and was showing the older woman the ropes, showing her the intricacies of taking orders and creating coffees with the espresso machine.

"Oh, I'll never figure all this out," the older woman said. "I can barely figure out how to feed my horses. I swear, I put three kids through high school and the whole time their homework was Greek to me. Just Greek."

She made some self-deprecating comment every time she was shown how to make an order, or to use the cash register to make change. And each time, the younger woman ignored her comments, and calmly and politely pressed on. At least a dozen times while I was there, in slightly different ways, the woman proclaimed her ignorance with a perverse and consistent pride. There were State of Jefferson brochures and newsletters on a side table and I listened to her while I read them.

It's notable that I saw two similar repeats of this performance- once at another shop in Etna, and another at the Seiad General Store. White middle-aged women proudly and almost defiantly proclaiming their possession of an abject ignorance while working behind windows with State of Jefferson seals on them. I mention it here not because I think those women were stupid or trying to lose their jobs, but that they seemed so secure. This puzzled me. I mean, the woman here in the coffee shop obviously wasn't hired because of any useful talents she had or any personal industry that would benefit the business, so how had she gotten the job? And how could she seem so confident that she wouldn't be laid off? Yet here she was, openly refusing to learn the shop's cash register and espresso machine. And there wasn't much else in there. Was it okay with the business owner if all she could do was turn on the microwave? It made me wonder about the business's owner. It occurred to me that seal on the window and the propaganda on the side table that couldn't have gotten there without the owner's approval.

There was a lot of pap about rights being trampled, and illegals flooding in through our insecure borders. Cities and counties on California's southern coast refused to enforce the nation's immigration laws so The State of Jefferson group was suing the state legislature to make them comply and to actively arrest and deport illegal immigrants. Their lawsuit had been dismissed by a liberal court, so they had started a Go-Fund-Me page to mount an appeal. While they were at it, they were planning lawsuits to repeal California's restrictive gun laws, among other things. 'Good luck with that,' I thought. The court they would appeal to was the Ninth Circuit.

The brochures and newsletters didn't seem all that aggressive, as I had expected them to be. It didn't seem like they were planning an armed rebellion. Instead, they seemed intent on pointing out to and reminding their readers of how they had been abused and looked down upon by Sacramento and the urban progressive elites on the coast. Their strategy to secede and escape progressive tyranny seemed to be lawsuit-based. By filing and losing lawsuits, and moving their way up the courts, they planned to prove to the Supreme Court that the northern Californians were hopelessly misrepresented in their own state's legislature, and that the only remedy would be secession. The Free and Independent State of Jefferson.

The propaganda didn't seem to be overtly racist either. There was no mention of ethnicities or race when they talked of illegals flooding into our country over the southern border. It was only implied.

But how would that propaganda get a foothold here? I was in a coffee shop 1,200 miles from the border. How many illegals, Hispanic or other, could there be streaming into and overpopulating their town? The town just wasn't that big, and I had walked all over it. The only Hispanic that I saw was Chameleon. It was weird.

Chameleon had told me that there had been a vocal minority that had agitated for splitting California up into two or three separate states for as long as she could remember. With 90% of California's population concentrated along the narrow strip on the coast, most of the state's political power and decision-making are made by those people that live in the urban areas. The people that live out in the country, and spread out over the majority of the state's land area, rarely have the ability to effect political outcomes. It breeds resentment. City life is different than country life, something I know firsthand from my experience as a country boy forced into the city to court my wife. City people look differently, behave differently, speak differently, and just think about things differently than people that have spent their lives out in the country. Not better, not worse, but definitely different.

I was raised as a country boy, so I know it's hard not to be intimidated in the city by city people. And I could see how resentment could grow in people who feel that their destinies are in the hands of the more politically powerful and populous people in the city that think differently than they do. It's hard not to think of yourself as an outsider for living out in the country, when politically, for all intents and purposes that's what you are.

One example of the stark differences in people's outlooks between city and country dwellers, is the notion of the zero-sum game. I was a country dweller the first time I ever heard the phrase, in a politician's speech. Bill Clinton started his speech explaining what it was, and I remember thinking, 'of course, that makes sense', and then continued through the rest of his speech telling me why I was wrong. Since then, city progressives have derided the conservative country folks' belief in the zero-sum game as it applies to economics and culture. And why not? To them there's no such thing.

In the city a reasonable influx of immigrants enlivens and enhances the city's culture and commerce. Immigrant entrepreneurs open auto body shops, upholstery shops, nail spas, and hair salons; they offer cheap landscaping, drive for Uber, and care for nursing home patients. In the city, immigration is not is not part of a zero sum game. New people and new cultures coming in enhances a city's vitality. But that's not how it works in a small country town. Think about it.

Imagine you live in a small town, with a population of 2,000 people or so. And you own a tire shop. Even though you own the only tire shop within a hundred-mile radius, you only make at best a modest living. There just aren't many people going through tires in your town. Now imagine that after 20 years selling tires, someone new moves into town and opens a new tire shop just down the street from yours. What do you think would happen? There's no room for innovation there, only a splitting of the already limited resources available. That's what a zero-sum-game describes.

City people and progressives are quick to point out the immigrants, especially illegal immigrants, are only taking the menial blue collar jobs that no one else really wants. But out in the country, away from the technology and banking centers, the menial and blue collar jobs are the only ones available, and they've been manned for generations by solid local stock. Out in the country the Zero Sum Game isn't a failed worldview. It's just the way it is.

I could understand the State of Jefferson secessionists' xenophobia. They may be defensive xenophobes, but for a lot of them, they had come by it honestly. The problem is that once your thought processes are moving down a xenophobic pathway, it's but a short and almost inevitable step to bigotry. I don't know how to change things, to soften up people's entrenched opinions when they have a sense of xenophobic victimhood to rationalize bigotry. I suspect Fox News and talk radio doesn't help, and I don't think labeling people as baskets of deplorables helps much either. Even if you don't agree you've got to have respect and give them a little. On the other hand, giving them Trump sure as hell hasn't helped.

I'm not the kind of writer that can be interesting while writing about insoluble problems. So I will stop now. I feel more comfortable describing things that I've seen, so I'll get back to that here.

Seiad Valley seems to be the heart of the State of the Jefferson movement. It figures prominently in the brochures and newsletters. Coming in, there's a big State of Jefferson sign alongside the highway, and another giant seal emblazoning the wall of the volunteer fire station. It's a tiny community, in a beautiful valley set amongst wooded mountains. It has a post office, grocery store, and restaurant alongside a lazy two-lane highway, all in the same building. The entire building isn't much bigger than an average sized country home. Chameleon and I had just finished shopping there, resupplying for the next section. The store's selection was small, so Chameleon had had trouble resupplying her food. For my part, I had pretty much cleaned out the store's entire stock of candy bars. We went outside to reorganize our groceries, remove excess wrapping, and pack everything into our food bags. We were outside in front of the post office, me on a bench and Chameleon sitting on the curb, when a big white farm truck came up the highway towards us and slowed as it approached. It was a flatbed, dual-wheeled, with diamond plate tool boxes and a farm fuel tank mounted on the back.

I watched the driver as he pulled off the highway and onto the shoulder, rolling slowly to park in front of the post office. I saw him look at Chameleon, and when he saw a purple-haired Hispanic woman sitting on the curb with a sack of groceries and a beat-up backpack his mustache lifted with an expression of disgust. He continued rolling in close, and as the passenger side door passed her, I saw him sit up higher in his seat to watch her in his side view mirror. He slowed to a crawl, and then stopped, exactly positioning the tail pipe of his big diesel truck right on top of her.

He revved the engine and watched in the mirror as a black cloud of exhaust belched out onto Chameleon. Then he got out of his truck, leaving the engine running, and walked around the front of it to pass by me instead of Chameleon on his way into the post office. He retrieved some mail, chattered pleasantly with a lady in the post office, and then came back out. Chameleon had moved to get away from the exhaust.

I couldn't think of anything to say so we just stared at each other a couple seconds. He wore blue jeans, cowboy boots, a white cowboy hat, and a western style shirt stretched over a pot belly that hung over a rodeo style belt buckle. He was mostly gray. Except for the belly and different clothes, he looked a lot like me. I still didn't have any words, but I didn't want to him leave thinking I condoned his actions either.

"I saw what you did there," I said.

He said nothing, just held my gaze a moment. Then he glanced over at Chameleon, smirked and got back in his truck. He pulled away, this time without revving or belching smoke. In the back window was an Independent State of Jefferson seal, sharing space with a Make America Great Again bumper sticker. I was still shocked by this stupid act of meanness, this senseless act of bigotry. I wondered if he was driving home to boast about it. I looked over at Chameleon.

"Hey," I said. "I'm really sorry about that." Chameleon didn't bother to look up. "Yeah," she said, "that just happens sometimes."

For the next couple of days I wanted to talk to Chameleon about it, it just felt like something else should be said, but I couldn't think of anything that would add any more in the way of clarity than Chameleon's initial explanation. 'That just happens sometimes.' Chameleon never brought it up either, the miles went behind us, and we never did talk about it again.

TICKS

Miles on Trail... 1,118

It looked like we had left earth behind as we came out of the forest. We had hiked somehow onto Mars, but not a completely barren Mars. It looked as though Elon Musk had been terraforming it.

"This is Dunite. That whole ridge is Dunite. That's nuts! Look how much there is, there's miles of it!" I said. We were going to be walking through it all day, at least.

"So what's Dunite?", Chameleon asked.

"This orangish rock that this whole area is made from. It's rare. Somehow it came up from the earth's mantle, from way down deep. Most rock comes from the earth's crust and is mostly silica. This stuff from the mantle has a lot of magnesium in it, so it's heavier. It's super hard too, and stands up to weathering better than just about any other kind of rock. Check it out." I handed Chameleon a rock.

"Yeah?"

"Yeah, the earth under our feet right now is probably like ten times older than the dirt on the rest of the trail. Feel how rough that rock is? It's so hard and crytalline that you can crush this up for industrial abrasives like for sandblasters or sanding discs, things like that."

"So what's that green rock over there?"

"More of it. It's green when you first crack it open, and then it weathers to this orange color. When it's green it's called Olivine. The black stuff," I said pointing to a streak, "is what they mine for abrasives. I'm surprised. We have a couple ridges of this Dunite back home in the Washington Cascades, it's fantastic to climb on and I always thought we had all there was of it in the United States. But this whole thing-everything we can see from here is Dunite. More than I've ever seen."

"I keep telling you, California has everything. And it's big", Chameleon said.

Dunite makes poor soil, and nothing grows very well in it. In the valleys, scraggly manzanita couldn't obscure the orange rock beneath. The peaks and ridges were clean orange rock streaked with black inclusions. Looking at it made my fingers twitch.

"I should climb this," I said, looking up a ridge.

"You should. You never do anything spontaneously. You're Mr. Make-a-Plan Follow-Plan. Boring. How does your wife put up with it?"

"Plan and Execute. I say what I'll do and then do what I say. There's nothing wrong with that. I'm Mr. Reliable."

"You're Mr. Boring. Dare you to climb that," she said.

I looked up the ridge. It was mostly broken rock scrambling with some trickier spots getting around or over some towers. It was doable. The ridge ended at a smallish summit to the north. There was another ridge trending from there westward that I could descend to get back on the PCT.

"Okay, how's this? I'll climb this ridge and then drop down that one and back to the PCT. That will put me an hour and a half behind you, but I should be able to reach the spring before you're done with lunch. If I can't make the summit up this ridge—"

"Ughh! If you're spontaneous then 'planning and execution' isn't involved, 'Mr. Reliable'. That's the essential definition of spontaneity. Ugh! Just do something and I'll see you sometime later. Jeesh!" she said, and walked off down the trail.

The climbing was pretty good going up the ridge, except for the places where I had to traverse sideways. Because I was wearing a heavy backpack, whenever I tried reaching out to the side for a hand or foothold the pack would tend to pull me out and away from the rock. 'Barndooring', it's called, when a climber loses his grip with a hand and foot on one side of his body and then hinges away from the rock. So I tried to just go straight up as much as I could.

From the top, I could see the trail stretching out ahead, but not where I had expected. Downclimbing the west ridge wasn't going to be the best way back. Instead there would be a ravine and some brush to negotiate.

It was a little brushy but I got back to the trail without tearing any clothes, coming out with just a couple skin scratches and scrapes. I took off my shoes to get twigs and stickers out of my socks and then hightailed it up the trail to catch up with Chameleon. I caught her just before the spring we were going to refill water and eat lunch at.

"So? How was it?" asked Chameleon. "Was it good?"

"The ridge was really nice," I said. "It was pretty brushy getting back down though. Hey I think maybe I got poked or something in the ribs here under my arm. It hurts a bit. Could you take a look at it?" I pulled my shirt up over my armpit and held my elbow up.

"Shit! Shit! Shit!," Chameleon shrieked. "You have ticks, and they're burrowing in! Quick, get your reading glasses and the tweezers out of your first aid kit. Hurry!"

I wondered why she needed my glasses as I rummaged through my pack for the tweezers. Chameleon wore contacts. Maybe she would use the lenses from my glasses to focus a spot of sunlight onto the ticks to back them out, I thought. She had just finished the Appalachian trail two years before, where ticks were common and I felt lucky to have such an experienced partner. It was a relief to be in such good hands.

I found the tweezers and turned around. Chameleon was standing with her back to me, topless and hugging herself.

"God, do I have any on me?" she asked. "And put your glasses on, I don't want you to miss any!"

"I'm the one with ticks," I said.

"Yeah, they're not going anywhere. We'll get to you."

Chameleon had beautiful brown skin. I couldn't help but think of the Jefferson State bigots from the country towns behind us. How could they be so afraid of having brown grandbabies?

"No ticks. You're clear," I said.

She shook out her sports bra and shirt, inspected them, and put them back on. "Ok, give me the tweezers, then," she said, turning around. She looked at the tick under my arm. "Hey, this is a big one. Looks like he's sucked up a lot of your blood."

"Well try to grab him close to my skin so you don't squeeze the blood from his stomach back into me. I think that's how you get Lyme disease," I said.

"Let loose, you little bugger," she said pulling on the tick. Then to me, "He's really digging in there."

"I took a wilderness medicine course a while back and I think you're supposed to use a steady pull, and maybe kind of roll him off backwards like. I think. Or maybe forwards. But I think backwards."

"Well that seems like an important enough point that you should have tried to remember it, don't you think?" she said.

"Hey, it was twenty years ago. What important points do you remember from when you were nine years old, huh?"

Chameleon laughed.

"Anyway, the one thing I remember for sure is that you need to be careful to not pull its head off. That would be bad."

"Hmm. Well, then it's too bad their heads aren't attached better," she said. "Because it just popped off and it's still in there."

"You have to get it out of there." Chameleon worked and worried on my skin with the tweezers. She'd push the open tweezers in towards my rib, clamp down on some flesh, and then yank it out. It didn't take too many times before it occurred to me that this might not be pleasant.

She squeegeed some blood off with the side of the tweezers to have a good look. "Missed again," she said, and went in again with the tweezers. All my hair was standing on end, and my teeth were gritted.

"You know, I'm surprised at how you can just stand there without flinching while I do this," she said. "I bet it hurts and you haven't sworn at me or anything."

"Yeah, well you should hear what I'm thinking right now," I said.

Chameleon laughed. "That is so funny. Maybe I'll post it." She squeegeed again. "Hmm. I think I got his head out with that one."

We instituted twice daily tick inspections and pulled several of them off each other over the next 100 miles. But none were burrowed in like that first one. Ticks aren't really very fast, and they like to move up your body a ways before burrowing in.

We came across a pair of middle aged guys hiking this section of the trail together, and having a miserable time of it. They were wearing full raingear tucked into socks and gloves, and sun hats chin-strapped over fully enclosed mosquito netting headgear. They were completely and uncomfortably 'tick-proofed'.

The days were getting warm now, up around 80 degrees in the afternoons. Hiking in the sun with raingear had to be someplace between torment and torture. But that's what you do if you don't have a partner for tick checks, I guess.

TURNING AROUND

Miles on Trail... 1,178

Cattle had been grazed in these uplands here in northern California since the turn of the century and there has been a stockman's cabin above this meadow for just as long. The Donomore Cabin is the second one to stand on the site, built in the 1930's. There was a guest register inside, some folding chairs, a scrapbook of pictures and newspaper clippings about the cabin and the family that owned it, and some musty blankets and clothes. The clothes were mostly children's snow suits, so snowmobilers must have come up for a visit. There was a child's Spiderman suit in the pile as well, complete with a pullover spidey mask and padded abs. Mice had been exploring it.

The sheet metal roof sagged but seemed water tight. Some of the panels had been replaced, the old ones had been torn off and left on the ground. The floor was crooked, and the walls were gapped so that you could see dust motes illuminated in the air. The place was standing but minimally maintained, in adherence to spirit of the name given to it. Donomore- Do no more. We had dinner, cooking on the cabin's front steps, then set up camp nearby.

This would be our last night in Northern California. Tomorrow we would be in Oregon, and the day after that, driving back to Truckee to hike south through the Sierras. The country was going to change; the terrain, geology, the animals and plant life all around. I had noticed that the ravens, who can live anywhere in the mountains had a different dialect here than the ones that lived in the southern desert. The southern California ravens gawked, clucked, and clacked when they talked to each other. The northern ravens were more sqawky and screamy. Things like that become more important when you are on foot, and you notice things like that, details of the biome you are walking through. It was all going to change soon.

"Do you think that two people, when they spend a lot of time together and then they don't, you know, and they go on their own ways? Do you think two people like that, would miss each other?" Chameleon asked.

"Well sure they would," I said. "That's just natural. I know when this is done and I can get back to my home and my family, I know I'll miss you." Chameleon was looking at me. "I'll miss you a lot. And that's okay. It's natural to miss people and think about them. If we never thought about other people, we'd all be pretty boring. Or psychopathic."

"I don't mind thinking of people, but I don't like missing them," Chameleon said. "It makes me sad. I had a boyfriend on Chuuk. You know, the island I was stationed on in the Peace Corps. I liked him a lot, but I knew that it would come to an end. He was an island boy, you know part of that culture and was going to stay on the island his whole life. When my tour was almost up, I started a fight with him."

"About what?" I asked.

"Well he stole some of my weed," Chameleon said. "It wasn't really the first time that he'd done that. In their culture personal property is sort of an iffy concept. And in their culture, pretty much anything that isn't nailed down belongs to whoever lays their hands on it. So to him it was really no big deal."

"So what did he do," I asked. "did he deny it or anything?"

"No he didn't deny it," Chameleon said. "And he did apologize. He apologized and promised to never do it again. He told me that in his culture, he had to do something to make me mad at him, so we could make up and be a real couple, and that was the only reason he did it. If I forgave him, he said, he'd never make me unhappy ever again."

"Do you think he loved you?" I asked.

"Yes, I think he did. It was sad, but I broke it off with him. Two weeks later my tour was up, and I went home."

"Do you ever miss him?" I asked.

Chameleon looked at me with liquid eyes. "Sometimes I think of him," she admitted. "And whenever I do, it makes me sad."

"You did what you had to do," I said.

"I know that," she said. "We're not going to talk about that again,"

We stopped at the Grouse Gap picnic shelter for our last night on the trail before Ashland. It was Father's Day, and as we walked up, a boisterous family arrived in three pickup trucks. They unloaded coolers and picnic chests of food, firewood for the shelter's central fireplace, folding camp chairs, and wrapped gifts. When they had set up in the shelter, Dave and Belinda the original instigators, were the twin centers of a binary system. Their two grown daughters and their husbands orbited about them near the shelter, and their two grandchildren followed eccentric, cometary paths of their own running into the surrounding meadows and back.

Belinda, with charcoals and sketchpad in one hand and a cane in the other, went out to one of the perigees to meet her granddaughter. Her granddaughter stopped running, and they sat together sketching flowers. From the shelter, they looked like a couple of sprites sitting together. Belinda wore a long natural cotton dress, leather sandals, sparkly eye shadow, and a narrow golden tiara. Her granddaughter wore a wolf-eared stocking cap over green Kool-aid colored hair with sparkles.

Her grandson, the girl's brother, was looking for beetles. When he found one, he'd run back to get his father, a nature photographer and his equipment. He would lead his dad back to the beetle's the general vicinity, and then search for it again. Her daughter, the children's mother, was a musician in a band that played mid-sized venues up and down the coast. Their summer tour was starting soon. Her other daughter was a chef, and had brought some pastries from her shop in Ashland. Her husband, dressed like an old-time cowboy, was an airline pilot. They didn't have kids; horses and trail riding took up all of their free time.

Chameleon went out to help search for beetles, and while the cowboy pilot and his wife got the picnic put together and spread out on the table, I helped Dave with the fire and chatted a bit.

Dave was a bit overweight, dressed comfortably in sweatshirt, cargo shorts, logger boot socks, and Romeo slippers. He's a retired danger-tree faller for forest service and fire crews. His job was to cut down the 'Burnin' Nasties'- trees that are already on fire so fire crews can get their equipment in and start fighting fires without having to worry about trees coming down on them. Wildfires usually are at their hottest relatively close to the ground where most of the dead and dying brush and branches are fueling it. So most of the damage to the trunks of the trees is done to the lowermost thirty feet or so. The trunks will often be 'cat-faced', burnt more deeply and severely on the windward sides by a fast-moving fire. It's extremely dangerous work, taking out burnin' nasties, because fire has weakened and unbalanced them unpredictably.

He spent most of his career falling burnin' nasties all around Seiad Valley. Most of that forest is burnt, and what's left is going to burn soon. When you're in the as yet unburned part, you can hear the bark beetles burrowing through and eating the cambium layer under the bark- eerie, alien snapping and clicking noises coming from the brown-needled trees all around you. They stop at night, start up again in late morning.

Dave and Belinda live in Yreka, the proposed capital of the state of Jefferson. Dave was cautious at first when he talked to me, the conversation tentative and probing, circling before he approached as if I were a burning nasty.

99

"In Yreka you need to be careful about airing your environmental views," he said. "But I think climate change is real, we did it, and we're living it now, right here."

I told him that I thought the wildlands and countryside here was beautiful.

"It is. There's nowhere else that I would have spent my life," he said, looking out on his wife and grandkids in the meadow. "But it is changing. We're getting isolated from the rains, the trees are drying up, and you can hear the beetles coming in, making the trees rotten and ready to ignite. It's going to rain a little tonight, but I'll tell you this: you're here at the right time. When you come back from hiking the Sierras, this place"- he looked around again at the land he loved, then back to me, "will be on fire."

THE RUBBER CHICKEN WALKS

Miles on the Trail... 1,248

Ten year-olds can fly on nonstop flights without their parents, so Monica had gotten Matthew onto the plane in Seattle. But now that his plane had landed in Reno, I didn't see him coming out of the jetway with the rest of the passengers. Where was he? I went over to the monitors again to make sure I was waiting at the correct gate.

"Hi, Dad." They had gotten Matthew off the plane first, and I hadn't seen him behind the ticket counter. He had dragged an agent over to get me. "What are you doing?"

We went to the baggage claim and picked up Matthews backpack. It had all the non-food items he would need for the next two weeks inside of it. More actually, as it turned out. Monica had added some extra clothing items that I hadn't put on the essentials packing list that I had sent them.

We go camping and hiking a lot, more than anyone else in our family. It's sort of our thing. There are three questions we're always asked about extended camping trips: What do we eat, How do we go to the bathroom, and How many pairs of undershorts do we bring. For the last, Matt and I have a stock answer, no matter how long the trip is. The answer is one pair of undershorts, and we explain it like this- Day one, wear your shorts like usual. Day two, you turn them inside out. Day three, turn them around. Day four, turn them inside out again. Day five, trade with your hiking partner and repeat as necessary. This always makes Monica gag and roll her eyes, which does nothing really but encourage us. Anyway, Monica made sure that Matt had enough underwear packed that he wouldn't have to share any with anyone that had been on the trail for the past three months.

From the airport we drove forty-five minutes to the hotel in Truckee, where Matthew met Chameleon for the first time. Chameleon was indulging in her pre-section hiking ritual, sitting on the bed watching Grey's Anatomy reruns on TV surrounded by the food she would eat for the next week. During commercial breaks, dramatic scene shifts, and other cues that I could never actually discern, she would alternately sort, shuffle, or scatter the food items around her. Then she would lie back and perform slow motion jumping jacks, sweeping her arms and legs to create an angel -shaped silhouette amongst the Pop-Tarts, gummy bears, and Slim-Jims. Then she'd sit up to sort, shuffle, and scatter her food on the bed anew. She liked to get to know her food well and have a personal connection to each item before lovingly stowing it in her bear can.

To me, food is fuel. So when I go shopping for trail food, it's not chosen for any purpose other than function. Not for its taste, ethics, sustainability, or any natural health benefits it may confer. Only function. I had fine-tuned my selections to meet three essential criteria; I got food I could sit on, that had lots of calories, and it only made me poop once a day.

I upended a grocery bag and dumped 96 Snickers and Payday bars onto the bed.

"What's that!?" Matthew asked.

"That's our food," I replied.

Matthew looked over at Chameleon, who was watching TV and nuzzling a Pop-Tart to her cheek. "What are we going to do with all these?"

"We're going to eat 'em. And turn them into poop."

"Why?" I couldn't think of short answer to summarize three months and 1,100 miles of trial and error diet experimentation on the trail. "Just help me get these into the bear can," I said.

A bear can is a plastic 3-gallon cookie jar with a child proof top that you put food into before going into the backcountry where the bears live. If a bear ever does get into a hiker's backpack, he won't be able to get the food out of the bear can. This way, bears learn that it doesn't pay to steal backpacks.

Chameleon had made arrangements to get a ride to the trailhead at Donner Pass with a trail angel at seven o'clock the next morning so everyone went to bed early that night. But the next morning, the trail angel had a different idea.

"I know a better place to drop you off," the Trail Angel said. "It's very scenic. I know you will love it!" So he dropped us off three miles from the trailhead. That made our first night's camp eighteen miles away instead of our planned fifteen.

There were a few patches of steep snow over the trail, but nothing Matthew couldn't handle. Matthew had had plenty of experience on steep snow hiking with me in the Cascades. The trick is to keep your body upright instead of leaning into the snow and to keep control of your ankles so that your feet make level, solid platforms in the snow as you walk.

It was hard work getting to the first night's camp, so hard that Matthew couldn't eat. He had only been able to eat two of the day's five Snickers he should have eaten to replace the calories he'd expended. Being at 8,000 feet elevation, and just coming from sea level the day before, eating a Snickers was the same to him as eating a truck tire.

"There's three more you need to turn into poop," I said when we reached our first campsite. "Get on it!"

Matthew took the remaining three snicker bars to a snowbank, unwrapped and arranged them to look like an irresponsible dog owner had been there. "How's that?" he asked.

The next day we traversed the ridge over Squaw Valley, the ski resort that hosted the Winter Olympics where Shaun White became famous. As we hiked, Chameleon told Matthew the story of the Donner Party, a group of immigrants that had tried to take a shortcut over the Sierra mountains in the Californian colonial days. They became lost and stranded and had to resort to cannibalism in order to survive. Chameleon had always thought that waiting for your teammates to die so that you could eat them was inefficient and wasteful. She thought it would be better to amputate and eat noncritical body parts as needed.

"If I had been in charge of the Donner Party," she said, "they all would have come out the other side in the spring alive, but armless."

"That's sick!", Matthew said.

Chameleon looked at him hungrily. "I would start with your left arm," she said.

"Want a Snickers?" Matthew asked. He was always trying to get rid of them.

Chameleon put on a maniacal expression, shook her head. Then in her best Smeagol voice said, "Wants meat!"

Matthew looked at his arm, thought a moment. "How many Pop-Tarts would you give me for it?"

From the ridge looking east was a good view of Lake Tahoe. From there the trail dropped in elevation to below the timber line and then into swampy areas that were infested with mosquitoes. Lots of mosquitoes. I had with me a little spritzer bottle of DEET, the same size and shape used for those little breath freshener sprays. But there just wasn't enough repellant in there to keep the mosquitoes off the both of us, and I ran out. Chameleon wasn't faring much better. Her repellant hadn't run out, but she was using an herbal-based repellent with questionable efficacy. It didn't do much to repel the mosquitoes, but it did pique their curiosity. Even though it was close to 80 degrees, we all had to put on extra clothes to keep from being eaten alive. Matthew wore my mosquito net hat while I spent a lot of time slapping my own face.

"Dad, How come you don't go to church with me and Mom?" asked Matthew. "Don't you believe in God?"

"Well I'm kind of undecided on all that," I said. "But I'm fine with you two going and I'm glad you do."

"So what do you mean you're undecided?"

"Well there's just a lot of questions that the church doesn't answer for me very well," I explained.

"Like what?"

"Well like these mosquitoes for example," I said. "If there's a God, why did he make mosquitoes? Why are they here?"

"Huh," said Matthew, "I see what you mean. I've been wondering that myself a lot lately," Matthew said.

Mosquitoes are awful. There's no getting around it. They can take a beautiful day and turn it to torture. We have mosquitoes at home in Washington, but they're seldom as voracious as the ones there in Northern California. In Washington the soil underfoot is almost always damp and puddled, so a mosquito can breed almost any time it wants to. But in northern California's mountains there's only a brief window when mosquitoes can breed. In the winter, the ground is covered in snow and frozen; then springs comes and seemingly instantly, the snow is melted out and the soil sun burnt to a dusty crisp. All the mosquitoes that want to breed have to do it all in that briefest of windows. And we were walking right through it. Our timing couldn't have been worse.

Female mosquitoes, besides male mosquitoes, need two things to breed. A puddle or damp soil to lay their eggs in, and a host for a good blood meal. The melting snow had made warm puddles and damp spots all around, perfect for incubation. And then here we came walking down the trail, full of blood, a feast for mosquitoes.

Hikers have several different strategies to avoid mosquitoes. Some try to hike at night and camp during the day, staying inside their tents during the warm hours when mosquitoes are the most active. Not only do they spend the hottest part of the day roasting inside their tents, the only scenery they enjoy is whatever their headlamps can illuminate for them as they walk through the darkness. Other hikers cover themselves from head to foot in clothing, rain gear, or mosquito netting. When you're dressed like that it's hot. Even mosquito netting ruins a nice breeze.

There are a lot of different mosquito repellents on the market that make their way to the trail. Chameleon did her best to stick with organic chemical-free mosquito repellents, and only used manufactured chemicals in extreme cases. I used a two-stage strategy myself. Stage one was hauling ass. Mosquitoes can't fly all that fast through the air. They are so small and their wings so feeble, that to them flying through the air is like swimming through asphalt is for us. As long as you can move more than about three and a half miles per hour, you can outrun most of the mosquitoes. There were some places where I couldn't go that fast, and other places where for one reason or another the mosquitoes were able to keep up with me, like if I had a tail wind. In those stage two cases I would bypass the organics and go straight for the chemicals; DEET 90% or more.

Any repellant that contains about 30% or more DEET will repel mosquitoes, but the higher the concentration, the longer it works. When you spray the higher concentrations on yourself your lips go worryingly numb. It also does strange things to plastics. I once wrecked a nice pair of sunglasses when I got DEET on them, but the mosquitoes stayed away.

In mosquito country, if you want to eat a lunch at less than three and a half miles an hour, it's best to eat inside a tent. For lunch that day, I dropped my pack and popped up my tent fly as quickly as possible, threw in my food bag and dove in after it. Matthew followed and then Chameleon, coming through like a fullback hitting the scrimmage line. We zipped shut the tent fly and spent a few frantic minutes inside the tent clapping mosquitoes. When you're hiking long distances, and have to sleep in your tent night after night, it's best not to smear mosquito guts all over the inside of it. It's best to get them in mid-air by clapping your hands.

The tent, exuding body odor and carbon dioxide from the three of us inside of it, became a powerful mosquito magnet. The cloud of them outside grew larger and thicker. There were so many mosquitoes that they affected the light level inside and the tent fabric took on a fuzzy appearance. They were poking their proboscises through, so desperate they were of getting to us.

We took turns exhaling through the tent fabric just underneath the mosquitoes. Our breaths would drive them into a frenzy, making them redouble their efforts to push their proboscises through and probe for blood. Then a hand quickly swiped across the inside of the tent fabric would mangle their little mosquito noses before they could pull them back out. We did this over and over again, neutralizing thousands of mosquitoes. It didn't seem to matter. When we emerged from the tent the mosquitoes fell onto us with the same intensity as before.

When we got to camp that night, Chameleon and I donned rain gear and set about making a smudge fire to fend off the mosquitoes while we cooked and ate dinner. When you hike most of the day at your own pace and alone it's nice to have some social time over dinner to catch up on the day's events, and chatting together around a fire is more satisfying somehow than shouting at each other from inside your tents. Matthew pitched our tent while Chameleon and I got a fire going and added damp sticks to make it nice and smoky. His clapping at the mosquitoes from inside the tent sounded like he was applauding our efforts.

Smoking yourself like pemmican jerky over a smudge fire isn't the best way to enjoy a meal. Matthew reasonably stayed put and had his dinner inside the tent while Chameleon and I asphyxiated ourselves outside. We finished up the meal as quickly as possible; I put the fire out while Chameleon hung the food bags for the night, then retreated into our tents.

A family of nighthawks came out and we could hear them chittering and diving to eat the mosquitoes above. Nighthawks are wondrous creatures. They are pigeon sized, with the wings of a falcon, but their mouths are more like a frog's. While they hunt they call out to each other with sharp, staccato vocalizations that they also use to echolocate and stun their insect prey. They'll make alarmingly swift dives after them with their frog mouths open wide, and then deploy their wings like airbrakes, making a whirring fluttery noise with each swoop back up. It's awesome to watch and magical to hear. A family of nighthawks whistling while they work.

As Matthew and I lay on our sleeping bags and chatted about the day, we could hear them above us. "So, Dad do you think God made nighthawks?"

Another bird made a dive and deployed his airbrakes while his family chittered and cheered him on. "Yeah, it sure sounds like it," I said.

"And they eat mosquitoes," Matthew said.

On the trail the next morning, Matthew made a discovery.

"Whoa! Look at this!" he said. He was holding a stick and looking at something on the ground. Chameleon and I came back to look.

There was a pinkish-brown worm thing limply lying on the trail. If it were stretched out it might have been three feet long. It was a little bigger around as a cat's tail, and didn't seem to have any eyes or mouth on either end of it.

"Is it alive?" Chameleon asked.

"Yeah. It moved when I poked it," Matthew said.

"Which way?"

"It didn't really go either way, it just sort of curled up a bit," he said.

"Do it again." Matthew poked the worm-snake with the stick again. It curled up again, and then started probing the ground around itself with both of its ends. It decided which way to go, and began slithering off the trail. Whether forwards or backwards, we couldn't tell.

"Is that his head then? Chameleon asked.

"I don't think so. It looks like it's backing away," I said.

After walking so long on a seemingly endless trail together, Chameleon and I came to relish any kind of trail oddity. We stared at if for a while.

Chameleon turned to me. "What the heck is that thing?"

"I don't know. I was going to ask you," I said.

"You're the environmentalist. You're supposed to know."

"You're from California. You're supposed to know"

"I know what it is!" Matthew announced. We turned to look at him.

"What is it then?" Chameleon asked.

"It's an Ed Zachary snake." "A what snake?"

"An Ed Zachary snake. Because its head looks Ed Zachary like its butt!" He held out the stick he was holding, and let go of it, drop-the-mike fashion. Then he turned and strode off down the trail.

Chameleon's friend and Appalachian trail partner was flying in to hike the next 140-mile section with her. We had to make at least seventeen miles each day to meet her in Tahoe, mosquitoes and Matthew's blistered feet notwithstanding. At one point on the trail, we took a wrong turn and ended up on a treacherous and steep slope above a cliff. We should have turned around immediately, but Chameleon and I decided to hang out for a bit to trundle.

Trundling is the act of tossing rocks down a steep cliff and watching them bounce. Trundling is hazardous, ill-advised, damaging to the environment, and highly illegal within national parks. But it's also cool to watch and a lot of fun. And sometimes, people just have to have fun you know?

"Look what I have," said Chameleon, holding up a football-sized rock.

"Chuck it! Chuck it good," I said.

She flung it over and we watched it clonk, chunk, clunk down the cliff. The rock bounded into space and rocketed downslope with alarming velocity. We could hear it slamming into trees after it had disappeared in the woods below, and there was the smell of ozone and gunpowder left behind it in the air.

"That was a good one," said Chameleon.

"Whoa!", I said. "That sucker did some damage."

There was one adult present at least. "I hope nobody was down there," Matthew said.

Our last camp for this section was on the shore of Dick's Lake, just below Dick's Pass. Matthew thought that these were the most hilarious names and drove me crazy making jokes about it.

"How many Dicks does it take to go over Dick's Pass?" he asked.

"I'm sure I don't know," I said.

"I don't know either." He giggled, gasped, and struggled with himself to blurt out the punchline. "Nobody does, *Because it's Dick's Pass!*" and dissolved into laughter.

When we reached Dick's Pass there was good cell reception. We called home with Duo and Matthew was able to get face to face time with his mom. Then he handed the phone over to me with instructions to keep the camera on him as he walked over to the wooden marker that read 'DICK'S PASS', and posed there with his hand over the 'P' in PASS.

"Hey Mom," he yelled. "See where I am?"

From there the trail continued downhill and into timberline to Echo Lake. Echo Lake was the edge of civilization, with fancy upscale cabins along shorelines and a boat that ferried people back and forth from the woods to the boat launch and grocery store at the road's end. We caught a ride into town, Chameleon to meet her friend and Matthew and I to regroup for the second half of our adventure.

THE RUBBER CHICKEN SWIMS

Miles on Trail.. 1,318

Matthew's feet were a mess. The shoes he had worn for the last week had slippery laces and as Matthew walked, the laces would slacken up down around his toes. Meanwhile, the tops of his laces would tighten like little nooses around his ankles. No matter how you tied the shoes to start with, a short distance later he would be wearing twin tourniquets as if we were getting ready to amputate. The tourniquets on his ankles would impede the return blood flow, so his feet were hot and swollen while they flapped around and abraded inside his loose shoes.

His ankle bones just above his shoes were barked up and bruised as well. The portion of the PCT that we had just walked, along the west rim of Lake Tahoe, was beautiful, and was the most heavily used portion of the entire PCT. And a lot of the trail showed the signs of its heavy use. In many places the trail was a deep rut. Meltwater and foot traffic had eroded the dirt and smaller pebbles out of the ruts, so that you were left walking on miles of irregularly shaped potato sized rocks. Footing in these ruts was difficult and as he walked, unpredictably a foot would roll off a rock that would flip up tiddlywink-like to bounce off his ankles. The plan had been to walk another 70 miles; it would be nearly a week before Monica would arrive. What to do?

There was a Big Five store in South Lake Tahoe, and we bought DEET and a new pair of shoes. Still, Matt wasn't keen to ride his feet for another seventy miles, new shoes or not. I couldn't blame him there. There was a kayak shop next door to Big Five. 'Hmm,' I thought. We went inside and chatted with the proprietor, an energetic and enthusiastic young man with a mop of curly wild hair. He had just opened his own shop that summer, selling and renting paddle boards and kayaks.

"Yeah, sure!" he said. "It's totally possible to kayak from the south end here all along the east shore to the north end of the lake. That would be such an epic trip! Let's see, that would be 75 miles or so. I'd drop you off at the Truckee River where it feeds Lake Tahoe. You'd paddle to the north end of the lake to the outlet, where the Lower Truckee starts. I'd rent you a double, like this green one here."

"When we get there, what would it cost for you to come pick up the boat?" I asked. "I don't think we could circumnavigate the whole lake."

"That's in a different county up there," he said. "I don't have a license to operate there out of my area, they're very strict about that around the lake. Also, I wouldn't want to close shop that long while I drove up there and back to get the boat. It's just me here, you know." His face fell.

"Well, my wife is flying in and is picking up a rental car. That would be six days from now," I said, thinking. "Do you have some of those little foam blocks and strapping you could send with us?"

"And you could bring the boat back here on top of the rental car! Awesome!"

"Well, she has a vacation rental in Truckee and I'd like to stay there a night or two, you know? And then I'd bring back the boat on the way when she drops me back off on the PCT. So I'd have the boat out for a little more than a week."

"Close enough!" he said. "We'll call it a week. Be here at 9:00 tomorrow morning?"

The next morning, he had a double kayak, complete with paddles, life jackets, dry bags, air horn, and other doo-dads already loaded into his truck. We piled in, and after a short drive we were at the starting point of our waterborne adventure. Seventy-five miles of paddling, five days on the water, four nights of lakeshore camping. We were excited about our new plans.

Matt and I spent some time re-arranging gear and food from our backpacks to stow inside the kayak. The bear can (of course, the hateful bear can) wouldn't fit in any of the storage compartments, so we ended up loosely strapping it to the back of Matthew's seat. Matt would have the front seat in the kayak, and I'd be in back.

"If I'm back here, it will balance the boat and I can steer better," I told him. Also, I liked the arrangement with the bear can full of candy bars behind him and within easy reach in front of me. I could sneak candy bars out and eat them while he paddled without him knowing. Matthew understood the implications of the arrangement immediately.

"Hey! You have all the candy bars in front of you. I need some in my go bag up here." A 'go bag' is a small bag that contains things you need ready at hand when you're on the go- things like sunglasses, lip balm, sunscreen. I was proud of him for thinking things through for himself instead of just relying on me.

"And there's no pee-bottles in this boat either," he said. "How's that going to work?"

Matthew has a lot of experience on the water in kayaks and rowboats back home. If you're in a kayak a long ways from shore, and you need to pee, you can't just stand up and go over the side. And if there are waves or swells of any size, you can't very well scooch yourself and your zipper over the side without capsizing either. At home, we always carried empty Gatorade bottles in our boats. If nature number one called, and we couldn't get back to shore, we'd pee in a Gatorade bottle between our legs and then dump it out over the side.

"You have extra water bottles up there. Just designate one as your pee-bottle," I told him.

"Give me one of yours," he said.

On a map, Lake Tahoe looks like the print of a giant's right foot. The Upper Truckee River runs into the lake at the south end, at its heel, so to speak, and the Lower Truckee exits at the north end, just at the web by lake's big toe where a sandal thong would go. We were on the river just south of the heel, and planned to paddle counter-clockwise around the outside of the foot, round the bays that made up the lake's the four little toes, and to meet Monica and her rental car at the lake's outlet. Here in the river we were alone with an assortment of sea birds. Tahoe is at about 7,000 feet in elevation, in the mountains. The Pacific Ocean is 200 miles to the west, apparently close enough for seagulls and sandpipers to have found their way there. Ducks, loons, and geese were also with us in the delta; I'm not sure if they were visiting or were permanent residents. We paddled downstream to the lake and turned right.

The paddling was nice. We hugged the shore, more or less, heading east. We had started in California, and we could see bike paths, skate parks, and picnic areas along the beach. There were other kayaks out on the water and people strolling along the beach. It was the right decision to get off the trail and onto the water.

The state line between California and Nevada was marked by a big black water pipe sitting on the bottom of the lake. The water was so clear that as we paddled over it we could see it reaching from the shore to far out into the deep. On the California side of the pipe were pedestrian-oriented parks and promenades; the Nevada side had casinos, hotels, and boutique shops.

We passed a couple lakeside hotels and stopped for lunch at an empty sandy beach, that turned out to be on the edge of a private golf and country club. There were grandstands erected beside the golf tees, and we could see golfers, presumably rich and famous, dressed smartly and walking with caddies on manicured greens. It was obvious that we weren't supposed to be there, but it was lunchtime, our bladders were full, and neither of us wanted to use the water bottles.

"Where are we supposed to camp?" asked Matthew.

"Well it doesn't look like we can camp here," I said. "Let's take another look at the map the guy gave us." There were no beaches ahead of us for quite a few miles. And no campground either. Nevada just isn't that much into campgrounds.

"Well there's a lot of rocky shore for the next couple miles," I said, "but here on the map there's a public boat launch within reach. I'm pretty sure we can get there before dark," I said.

"So you want us to camp at a boat launch?" Matthew asked.

"No, I don't really want us to," I said. "But it looks like that's what we're going to do."

The guy from the kayak rental had told us that Lake Tahoe usually had calm mornings that make for easy paddling, and got progressively windier through the afternoons and evenings. He had recommended that we get up early each morning and start paddling at daybreak. If we could get to our next campsite by noon we could avoid waves and choppy water. You tend to appreciate calm water when you are paddling a kayak. The wind was coming out of the west, and it freshened up a bit as we paddled. Since we were paddling along the east shore, and the wind was coming out of the west, there was a lot of fetch. Fetch is the amount of open water that wind can blow unimpeded across to make waves. So we were paddling along the fetchiest part of the lake.

As the waves picked up and the paddling more demanding, I became more and more aware of how my arms had begun to atrophy. I hadn't done much of anything with my arms for the last three months on the trail, and I was feeling it now. I told Matthew to paddle harder, and then surreptitiously stopped paddling to let him do the work to propel us forward. These breaks were short however, because Matthew always caught on after just a few strokes.

We paddled another eight miles past beautifully situated waterfront homes with dinner party patios to the shore's edge and docks or piers poking out on the water. Speed boats and jet skis were held up above the chop in cradles that could be lowered into or lifted out of the water. Some of the piers were up on their pilings high enough for us to paddle under. But most of the time we stayed out from shore far enough to get around them.

The Cave Rock boat launch was the only publicly-owned land along this stretch of Tahoe's east shore. It was a pretty ridiculous place to camp. Cave Rock is the solid rock shoulder of a mountain that lifts straight up out of the lake. There is no beach, or flat area of any kind, just a nearly vertical towering rock wall. There was no way to build homes on it, and even worse, no way to build a road on it either.

So in the 1930's when Highway 50 was built along Tahoe's east shore, they had to bore a tunnel through the rock. The first tunnel was 150 feet long and just wide enough for two lanes. When the road was widened to four lanes in the late 1950's another tunnel was bored through, this one deeper into the mountain's shoulder.

This one is 450 feet long. Boring out the tunnels made a lot of rubble that needed to be disposed of so it was dumped nearby, in the lake. There was enough rubble to build a parking lot big enough for a hundred boat trailers on top of it. A jetty and double lane boat launch was built at its north end, a tiny beach and a single picnic table at the other.

Cave Rock was sacred to the native Indian tribes, and they weren't very happy about having tunnels bored through it for a highway or having rubble land-filled into the lake below it. To demonstrate their sensitivity to the Indians' heritage, the Nevada Department of Transportation responded. They posted signs prohibiting rock climbing on Cave Rock near the bore holes and others prohibiting overnight camping at the parking area built atop the rubble they had dumped in the lake. When the boat launch toll booth closed at 8:00pm, I began to set up our tent next to one of the signs.

"We can't camp here. The sign says 'Absolutely No Overnight Camping Allowed'," Matthew said.

"Yeah, I saw that."

"Then we can't camp here. That's what the sign says."

"So, does it mean absolutely no overnight camping allowed ever? We've been camping overnight for the last week. Do you think that wasn't allowed?" I asked.

"That was way over on the other side of the lake, miles from here," he said.

"Ed Zachary," I said. "The sign doesn't mean absolutely no camping allowed anywhere, then. Camping was okay over there."

"Yeah. The sign wasn't over there."

"See? We weren't disobeying the sign when we were over there because we were outside of its circle of influence. The sign's authority is limited by distance."

Matthew was following my logic. "What?" he said.

"That sign has a circle of influence, right? It doesn't mean no camping allowed in the whole world, or no camping on the PCT, just no camping within its circle of influence. It only has authority within its circle of influence, see? So the question is, just how wide is its circle? We just need to camp outside of that."

"Well how wide is it?" asked Matthew.

"I don't know. Put your arms out and spin around like a helicopter. Everything you hit is inside your circle of influence. That's where you have authority."

"So we only need to camp farther than arm's reach from the sign?" "That's what I'm thinking. I'm setting up right here."

Matthew looked at me narrowly. "So just how wide is your circle of influence?" he asked.

The dangerous thing about leading Matthew partway down a path of logic is that he'll continue to follow it on his own for far longer than what I believe is productive. I needed to set him straight.

"My circle of influence is vast. In fact, my authority encompasses the entire Milky Way galaxy," I said.

Matthew paused a moment to check my assertions against prior observations. "I'm telling Mom," he said.

We packed up camp and were back on the water before the boat launch opened in the morning and looked up as we rounded the buttress of Cave Rock. It rose impressively straight up from the depths of the lake. Beyond Cave Rock the terrain above the lake still remained steep and bouldered, with no beaches. There was no place to land the kayak so a disagreement broke out about whose water bottle was to get used since we couldn't get to shore. The map showed small beaches about ten miles ahead, and I was anxious to get there early before the forecasted winds materialized. Better yet, the map showed that this was government-owned property, BLM land, so I knew we could camp there with no private residences or park rangers to bother us.

On the way we saw something floating on the water and paddled over to find a broken Super Soaker. Matthew stowed his paddle and spent the next hour or so fiddling until he got it to work. It was beautifully sunny, and the afternoon wind was just beginning to wake up when we got to the beach. We pulled the kayak up onto the sand, stretched and checked for cell service. We didn't have enough bars to make a Duo call but it was really nice to hear mom's voice. We put her on speaker phone and chatted for a bit sitting on a log up on the bank overlooking our kayak on the beach. As we talked squirrels came out of the brush, climbing all over our kayak deck and into the forward storage hold.

When Matthew was done talking with his mom he went back down to the beach, filled his Super Soaker and pulled a Payday bar out of the bear can. He peeled a couple peanuts off the Payday bar and placed them on the forward hull of the kayak. Then he stationed himself behind some driftwood with his Super Soaker and waited. It was nice having a chance to talk to Monica. We talked about family, and parenting things, and then of course the house and its never-ending remodel. Since I had left, Monica had been handling all of the remodeling and contracting herself. There were a lot of issues that she was dealing with on a daily basis without me.

I couldn't see Matthew from where I sat, but I could see the peanuts on the kayak. A squirrel hopped up on to the hull, sat on his haunches, picked up a peanut in his paws and began nibbling on it. A stream of water jetted out from the right, hit the squirrel just below his ear and toppled him over the side of the kayak. Laughter exploded from the water jet's source. Matthew continued reloading peanuts and washing squirrels as Monica and I talked. A pleasant and relaxing way to spend the afternoon.

I heard a noise coming from the trail behind me, and looked up to see a man coming down the trail to the beach. He had taken his clothes off and wrapped them in a towel that he carried under his arm. I heard more voices coming from behind him, some male, and some female.

"Well, it looks like we have company. And it looks like this might be a nude beach or something," I told Monica.

"A nude beach? Why did you take our boy to a nude beach?"

"It wasn't a nude beach when we got here."

"Well it sounds like it is now," she said. "You'd best take Matthew somewhere else."

I hung up the phone and as I went down to the beach, met Matthew coming up towards me wide-eyed.

"There's a guy here with no clothes on," Matthew whispered. "What's he doing?"

"I think this might be a nude beach," I said. "We should probably find someplace else to go."

We quickly re-stowed our gear back into the boat, and donned our life jackets. We had pulled the boat up the beach nose first, so now pushed the boat backwards down the sand till it was partially floating in the water. I climbed in my seat and watched the people clotheslessly deploying themselves behind Matthew on the beach. Matt worked to push the boat farther back into the lake, climbed in, and said, "That should be illegal."

Matthew, now seated in the boat, was faced by a half dozen nude sunbathers. One guy was already sitting on his beach towel with his feet towards us, and our view looking upslope was something a ten year-old would have trouble trying to unsee.

"Gross! All those people should be in jail!" Matthew said. He was pushing us off the sand, frantically using his kayak paddle as a pike pole.

"That guy probably should," I conceded. Matthew had backed us off the beach and the kayak was floating free. "But it's a free country and"-

Done with poling, Matthew pirouetted the paddle above his head like the rotor of an attack helicopter. The sharp edge of a carbon fiber paddle blade cut the bridge of my nose.

"Jeez!" I yelled. "What the heck are you doing?"

"Getting the heck out of here." His paddle blades were now two splashy blurs and a wake veed out from the nose of the boat.

"I'm back here bleeding." Matthew kept back-paddling us away from shore.

"So? You said there's no sharks in Lake Tahoe. Now turn this thing around."

We paddled past rocky shores another three and a half miles further to Sand Harbor State Park. It had a long sandy beach below a rocky point, fairly filled with people and beach umbrellas. The afternoon wind was up with a bit more intensity than we had seen, and teenagers were diving under or body surfing in the waves. We pointed the bow at a landing spot on the beach, and paddled furiously as a particularly energetic wave came up behind us. We rode the last twenty yards in on the wave and it pushed us far up onto the beach, scattering kids and nearly destroying a sand castle. We pulled the boat up through the sand and stashed it amongst the bushes above the beach and set out to explore.

Sand Harbor State park hosts a summertime Shakespeare Festival in an amphitheater backed by the beautifully clear lake and the mountains beyond. There are excellent picnic and group area facilities near the amphitheater as well as a concessionaire-run restaurant that serves burgers and ice cream. There are day use picnic tables spread out over 50 acres of pine woods, connected by winding walking paths. What it doesn't have is overnight camping. The Sand Harbor State park is day use only. No camping allowed. There were plenty of signs posted informing us of the fact.

"Here we go again," Matthew said.

"Yeah, I know. You don't have to say it," I said.

"This wouldn't happen if Mom was here."

"I said you didn't have to say it, didn't I?"

It was obvious that stealth camping here would require a higher level of stealthiness. Park rangers cruised the concrete walking paths on ATV's, patrolling the picnic areas, watching barbecues, and emptying trashcans. We went to get hamburgers and ice cream to make a plan.

We took our food to the outside food court and watched as a family of five fed French fries to a couple of squirrels. One of the squirrels was positively gargantuan, and the other merely fat. Both of them were bold enough to take French fries from the children's' hands. The fat squirrel would take a French fry, bite it into chunks small enough to stuff into his cheeks, and then dash up a picket fence, jump to a tree trunk, and disappear into the branches above somewhere. Then he'd come back down, cheeks emptied, and beg for another fry. His super-sized friend stayed behind on the ground. Every fry he got, he ate on the spot.

Reconnoitering, we found a good tent site hidden up against the boundary fence on a service road behind a picnic table. We brought our things from the kayak, making a couple trips to do it. We couldn't afford to be seen walking around with tent pads or sleeping bags strapped onto the outside of our packs in full view.

The wind didn't abate that night, and the next morning three foot waves were breaking on the beach. We launched nose first, quickly between waves. Still one came over the bow, soaking Matthew. He used a water bottle to bail as I paddled into the wind.

Three miles of rocky shore and wind exposure lay before us and the sandy and wind protected beaches of Incline Village, situated on the 'toes' of the giant's footprint outlined by Lake Tahoe. The waves grew stronger and steeper sided after we rounded the point above Sand Harbor, and we couldn't continue to hold to a northerly course with the waves coming broadsides to us. Instead, we had to quarter into the waves at an angle going out and away from the shore. We'd scratch and claw our way out into the waves till we were a quarter mile or so from shore, then just as we perched on the top of a wave, quickly turn the boat ninety degrees to the right and paddle hard. It wasn't as windy or bumpy on these downwind legs, but was definitely more nerve wracking. Even paddling as fast as we could, we couldn't match the speed of the waves and they'd come up from behind, trying to push us off course. It was hard work steering the kayak; if I were to slow down or let a wave roll us too far to the side, the next wave would surely broach and capsize us.

We had zigzagged about two miles up the coast when Matthew said, "I want to go to shore now."

"There's no shore to go to," I said. "It's all rocks and froth along there."

"What I have to do, you don't want me doing in a water bottle," he said.

"What? Why didn't you do it back there where we had flush toilets?"

"I didn't have to then. Now I do."

"You're killing me"

"You're feeding me Snickers and Payday bars," he retorted.

A few more zigzags got us past the bus-sized rocks lining the shore and we were able to land on a thin ribbon of sand. A wave pushed us all the way up the sand and flotsam at full tilt and crashed us into the brush at the top of the beach's slope. Two more waves came over the back deck and partially swamped the kayak before we could pull it farther up and into the brush. Matt clambered up the steep bank somewhere with the toiletry camp bag while I bailed out the boat and battled with the scrubby vegetation to get the boat turned around and ready to relaunch into the surf. When Matthew came back, I outlined the relaunch plan.

"Okay, we're going to get a little wet," I said, "until we get out away from shore a little ways. The slope here is steep enough for both of us to get in the boat here and then slide down into the water. Here, I've got your sleeping pad out. Put this over your lap like a spray skirt. Kind of hold it up with your knees, see if you can keep most of the water from getting into the boat. Once we're launched, I've got to paddle hard to keep us pointed that way into the upwind leg so you'll have to bail yourself. If I quit paddling to help, we'll get sideways or get smashed into those boulders there. Got it?"

The plan excited his spirit for adventure. "Do I have to?" he asked.

"You *get* to," I enthused. "Just think how awesome this is. I'll bet none of your friends have done anything like this. Besides, what's the worst that can happen?"

Matthew has heard me ask this question hundreds of times. It's sort of a parenting thing I've done consistently with him since before he could talk. I believe it's important for children to practice situational awareness, to notice the environment around them and to predict the possible consequences of their actions within it. If your child can answer "What's the worst that could happen?" you know that he has actively observed his immediate surroundings. He has formulated possible courses of action to take, and has analyzed their probable outcomes. This exercise helps them feel prepared, and gives them confidence.

Matthew looked out at the whitecaps, observing, formulating, and analyzing. Gaining confidence. "I think we should call Mom first to tell her we love her," he said.

We pushed off down the sand. The first wave went over the hull and broke over the sleeping pad in Matthew's lap.

"This isn't working!" Matt yelled.

"We need to get out there," I yelled. "Keep pushing!"

We got launched off the beach, but we had taken on a lot of water. The front end of a kayak isn't bulkheaded; it needs to be open so that the person in the front seat has someplace to put their legs. This open space had become partially filled with water, and the extra weight up front made the kayak heavy and sluggish. The bow became reluctant to rise with each successive wave.

It was difficult paddling to keep us from broaching and Matthew was busy up front, trying to hold his sleep pad in place when the wave crests came over and then bailing in the troughs in between. But the water was winning, coming in faster than he could bail it out. The boat rode lower and lower in the water until the bow refused to rise at all. Instead it stayed level and the bow of the boat disappeared into the base of a wave. Green water hit Matthew's chest full on.

"Well, I'm outta here," he said matter-of-factly, and jumped overboard.

I was left sitting alone in a kayak submerged six inches underwater. There was nothing to do now but follow his lead. The beach we had just left wasn't far off so we went there, sitting and shivering in the wind, waiting for our boat and scattered supplies to wash ashore.

Most of our things were either stowed in the rear bulkhead or sealed in water-tight drybags, so it was nice to be able to change into dry clothes. We gathered all our things back together, and turned the boat upside down to get the water out. Neither of us were keen to try the experiment again, so we pulled the boat partway up a tree and tied it there.

We scrambled up the steep bank to the footpath Matthew had found earlier, and followed it to the highway and turned left. We walked two or three miles to the sedate and moneyed Incline Village to a bus that took us to Knight's Beach, with a more touristy and boisterous atmosphere, and played a couple rounds of mini-golf and ate some ice cream cones before I let Matthew have the phone. I wanted him to be in a more positive state of mind before calling home.

"Hey Mom," he said. "Guess what Dad did to me this time."

END OF PART ONE

* * *

COMMENTS FROM HALFWAY HOME

If you've had the fortitude to stay with me and read this far, thank you. I really appreciate it. You probably haven't learned much of importance, and it's doubtful that your life has been much changed either. And that's okay, so long as we both understand and accept this together.

I do hope you were mildly entertained though. Hiking the Pacific Crest Trail was the single most enjoyable, healthy, interesting, and at the same time, most pointless, selfish, and unproductive thing I've ever done in my life. If you've ever thought about hiking it yourself, I whole-heartedly recommend going. Even if you would have to move heaven and earth in order to do it, do it.

Now, as far as this book is concerned. Fully half of the trail is left to do as this short book ends. So you may be wondering- did I finish the trail, and if so will I write about it? The answers to both are 'yes'. I had set myself a deadline to get this done and out, and as I'm typing this the deadline has drawn near. I'm a slow writer, and only a part-time one at that, and I need to get a few things done around here before my family throws me out. I've spent a great portion of the last couple months around them only half-aware and absent-minded, constantly typing upstairs or editing passages in my head. The second half of the adventure is outlined and blocked out. Besides, there's no chance I'd forget any of it anyway. There will be a Book Two. Soon I promise, I'll get back to it. And I hope you will too.

Thanks so much for reading so far.

IN THE PACK

A few folks were wondering what all I carried in my pack. The following pictures are photos from the planning stages of everything I was going to wear or put in my backpack. During the hike, I made some substitutions.

Walking clothes...

Darn Tough socks, thin liner socks, Smartwool base layers, and Value Village shorts. Kuhl baseball cap, a cotton handkerchief, and a Buff tube (you wear it on your head), Trekking Poles

Added: None

Sent Home: Baseball cap

Replaced: Shorts with a No-Belt, smooth waistband version; SmartWool boxer briefs with cotton version.

Packed Clothes...

In good weather, these clothes stayed in my backpack. A rain coat, pack rain cover, a rain kilt, and a down jacket. Extra socks.

Added: Three pairs, ankle high liner socks. One pair designated as sleeping socks

Sent Home: None

Replaced: None

Navigation and communication...

HalfMile's paper maps, a Silva Ranger Compass, Garmin InReach GPS, External Battery, Samsung Galaxy 7 smartphone, Yukuma external battery that can be recharged in 30 minutes

Added: Phone Apps, Guthook's, HalfMile's, Earthmate
Sent Home: Paper maps
Replaced: None

Sleeping Arrangement...

A sleeping quilt (like a bag without a bottom side), a sleep sack that's washable, a NeoAir pad, and my favorite blanky.
Added: None
Sent Home: None
Replaced: Sleeping Quilt for a Sleeping Bag for the cold and wet parts of the hike.

Camping Set...

A Sierra Designs tent that's held up with trekking poles, camp slippers, pocket rocket stove, and water treatment. Titanium cookpot, cup, and spork. Two lighters, camp towel, water bag, water bottles, 80 feet of parachord
Added: None
Sent Home: Cup, Large water bottle
Replaced: Lightweight Tent for the wet and cold parts of the hike

Toiletries and Miscellaneous...

Headlamp, dental floss, pocketknife, Kleenex, hand sanitizer, WetOnes pack, toilet trowel, mini flashlight, sunglasses, reading glasses, journals, pen, first aid kit, sewing kit, duct tape and athletic tape wrapped around water bottles, travel size toothbrush and toothpaste.
Added: None

Sent Home: Large journal, Kleenex, Hand sanitizer, coban wrapping
Replaced: None

Food...

None of what I started with worked. I had bought a Kevlar UrSack, a food bag that bears can't chew through. But even though they can't chew through the Kevlar and rip the bag open, they can use it for a chew toy. Their use is illegal through the Sierras; bear cans are required. And the food I started with had me losing too much weight to be sustainable. This is what I ended up eating daily on the trail:

Breakfast: 2 Met Rx BodyBuilding bars
Before lunch: 4 Snickers bars
Lunch:2 Don Pancho large flour tortillas, peanut butter; 1 Snicker bar
After lunch: 4 Pay Day bars
Dinner: Knorr Rice Side, with added cheese and/or summer sausage, and Idahoan Instant Potatoes for thickening. Hills Bros Café Vienna

About the Author-

Rick had been hiking, backpacking, and mountain climbing for fifty years before stepping out onto the Pacific Crest Trail. He started life as a bratty kid in southern California, then then moved to Washington to be a farm boy in Raymond, then a dairy farmer in Skagit County. After spending the first half of his life getting milk out of cows, he sold his herd and returned to college. Since then he's taught Backcountry Travel, Mountain Climbing, and Cartography at the junior college level. His full-time gig is working with fish and wildlife; spawning fish, and tracking elk. He lives in Conway, Washington with his wife Monica and son Matthew, the Rubber Chicken.

Made in the USA
Middletown, DE
19 July 2019